SONG ATLAS

SONG ATLAS

Andreas Ströhl

Translated from the German by
Amy Kardel

ELBORO

SONG ATLAS
Copyright © 2023 by Andreas Ströhl

All rights reserved. No part of this book may be used or reproduced in any manner whatsoever without written permission except in the case of brief quotation embodied in critical articles and reviews.

ISBN: 978-1-7379274-8-8

Published in New York by Elboro Press

Elboro Press books may be purchased in bulk for educational, business or sales promotional use. Please address enquiries to:

office@elboropress.com

First Edition, 2023 – Second Printing

CONTENTS

Introduction - *vii*
Kansas City - 11
New Orleans - 21
Atlanta - 43
Birmingham and Alabama - 57
Baltimore - 79
Mississippi - 95
Chicago - 125
Texas - 147
Los Angeles - 167
San Francisco - 195
St. Louis - 211
Memphis - 223

INTRODUCTION

"The only thing good about America is peanut butter," Janis Joplin supposedly said. There is probably some truth in this quip but while it is clear there is a great deal of hardship in the US and missed opportunities, in addition to great peanut butter there are also friendly folks, amazing landscapes, and wonderful music. The connection between the land and its music is exceptionally strong. *Song Atlas* focuses on this close connection between the land, the cities, and the music.

Globalization has garnered much attention for good reason. Yet nothing about it is a surprise. Much more astonishing is the hardy persistence of local regionalisms. One hundred years ago, people thought that the rise of radio would mean the end of dialects within two generations, the radio would be a relentless neutralizer of all regional phonetic peculiarities. But today a visit to Huntsville or Boston quickly proves the opposite. One could call this cultural persistence resilience, a strong local identity, or even love of place. These regionalisms coexist with industrial pop music, which is nearly globalized, just like Hollywood produces films for the entire world with help from top talent from around the world.

Popular music is often regressive. It mourns the past while simultaneously mourning a present that has yet to be. It conjures a sentimental reflection of a coming future in the here and now, awakening a sense of loss. And it recycles. Many blues, R&B, folk, and rock texts from the 1960s and '70s are composed of recurring elements that often retain little meaning as they are reused in respective combinations. They often point to something well known, such as when Bob Dylan's early ballads reference Scottish or Irish predecessors or the Rolling Stones riff off Robert Johnson or Jimmy Reed. Popular traditional music is a referencing system, almost hermetic to outsiders. But it is also a navigation and orientation system to guide informed listeners across broad landscapes.

For instance, the "Texas River Song" reveals a complex web of waterways across the Lone Star State:

> *Now the girls of Little River*
> *They're plump and they're pretty*
> *The Sabine and the Sulphur*
> *Hold beauties a many*
> *On the banks of the Neches*
> *There are girls by the score*
> *But down by the Brazos*
> *I'll wander no more*

"Texas River Song",
traditional, first publication 1942

Gaston Bachelard and Yi-Fu Tuan employed the word "topophilia" to refer to "positive affective ties with the material environment, a personal relationship to a beloved place." Topophilia is not an anomaly, even if it sounds like hemophilia or some other serious illness. Janis Joplin grew up in Port Arthur on the border between Texas and Louisiana, with peanut butter and Southern Comfort, the sweet whiskey liqueur with a lovely name. The South needs comforting still. It has needed comfort since "The Night They Drove Old Dixie Down" and "all the way from New Orleans to Jerusalem." Since then, "freedom is just another word for nothing left to lose," somewhere between Baton Rouge and Salinas....

What is this magic of sung and mumbled words naming places?

This book is a journey from East to West or West to East across, mostly, the southern US. I can "say I've been hittin' some hard travelin' too." That is the program Bob Dylan cast as his life project in his "Song to Woody" with reference to his friend and role model. That was in 1962, at the very beginning of his career, the year I was born.

Today, Dylan is still on his never-ending tour. Before and while I was writing this book, I, too, traveled extensively and excessively all over the South. I have been almost everywhere, and that gave me indescribable joy and pleasure

> *I've been everywhere, man*
> *I've been everywhere, man*
> *Crossed the deserts bare, man*
> *I've breathed the mountain air, man*
> *Travel, I've had my share, man*
> *I've been everywhere*

"I've Been Everywhere"
Geoff Mack, 1959

This book is a selection of just a few of the thousands of possible regional tours in song. The only criterion for inclusion of a song was my subjective judgement and preference. And perhaps the omission of songs that are all too well known about cities who get all the songs. We have not heard enough about Birmingham, Alabama, and especially about East St. Louis. We will not explore a rhapsody about Times Square but prefer to hear about *a place called Okfuskee*. We press a microphone into the hand of the "fat of the land," let it sing, and listen closely. And with a bit of luck, we will receive a gift in return. The result is a kind of atlas that is no less informative and precise than Rand McNally's "Road Atlas".

Just take the lyrics seriously and listen to the music. Then you will have been everywhere as well.

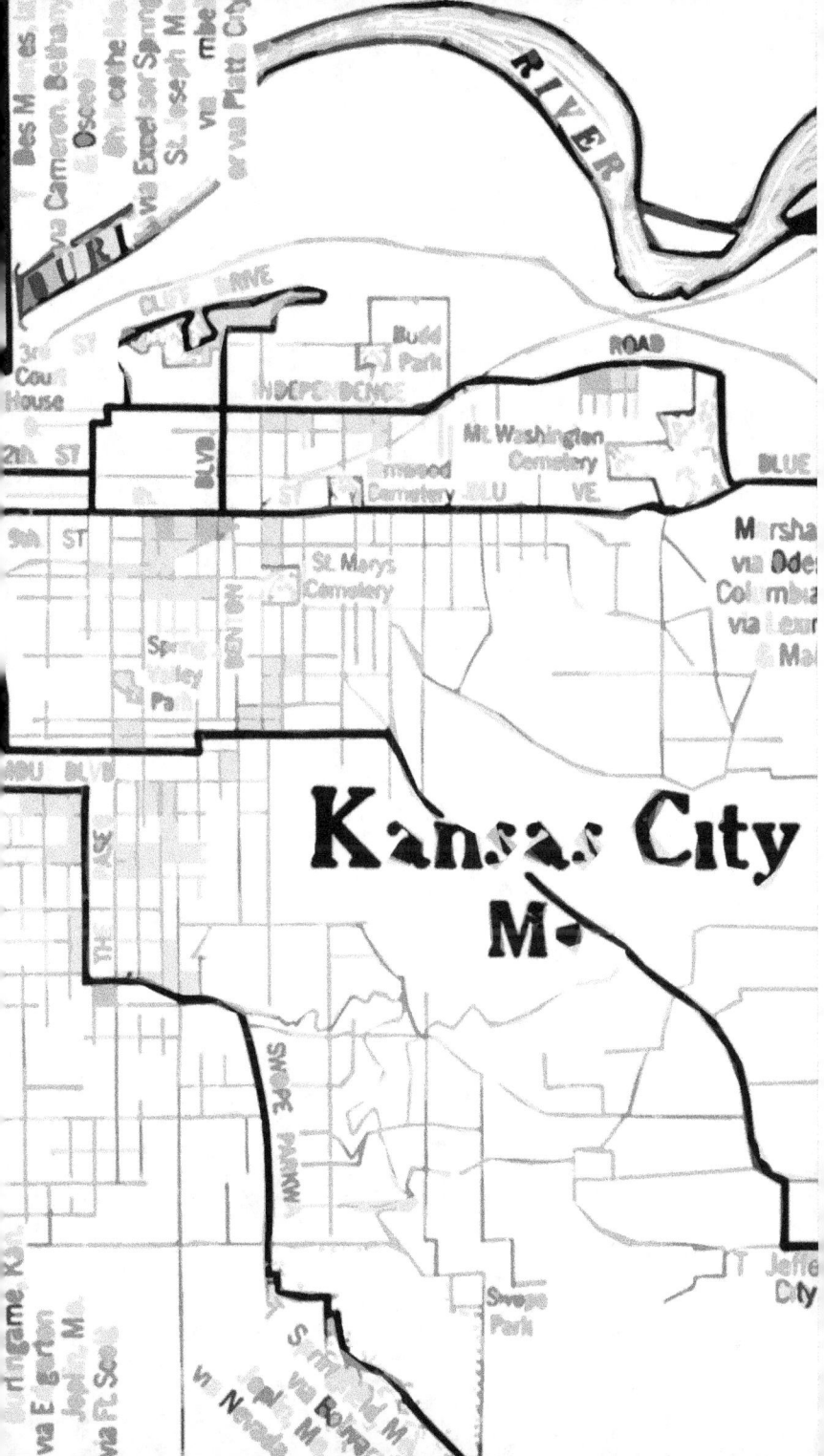

KANSAS CITY

Starting in Kansas City may seem unusual for a journey tracing the pop music of the American South and its cultural history, but I have my reasons. My personal connection to this city began in Munich, Germany, in 1976, with the song "Kansas City".

I began listening to rock'n'roll when I was fourteen years old, checking out music cassette tapes from the Munich City Library. The first one I brought home was Bill Haley's version of this song. I remember not being able to get that driving beat of his out my head during my confirmation.

> *I'm going to Kansas City,*
> *Kansas City here I come!*

"Kansas City"
Jerry Leiber and Mike Stoller, 1952

One year later, at the age of fifteen, I formed a garage band that I still play with today, forty-five years later. And, of course, I was still playing with that band when I actually got to Kansas City for the first time. *Well, I might have taken a train, I might have taken a plane, but if I had had to walk, I'd have been going just the same.* I was finally going to Kansas City, *Kansas City here I come!*

> *I'm gonna be standing on the corner*
> *of Twelfth Street and Vine*
> *With my Kansas City baby*
> *and a bottle of Kansas City wine*

So, in 2017, I was finally standing on the corner of 12th Street and Vine, albeit sans a Kansas City baby. There were more big issues: Wilbert Harrison, the immortal singer of "Kansas City", who only had two hits, had been dead for twenty-three years and Kansas City wine was hard to procure. I finally found a few suspicious looking, over-priced bottles in a large grocery store. The manager himself advised me not to buy them. I took his advice. I'd already tried a few revolting Missouri wines and didn't want go down that road again. I suspected labeling the bottles, "Kansas City Wine," was purely an attempt to rip off fans of the song.

This suspicion lingered as I searched for the street corner memorialized in the song. As a consequence of a downtown revitalization effort, 12th Street and Vine no longer intersected. After cruising around for a long time, however, I found a small park where 12th Street used to be. I parked my car in a weird little parking lot painted like a giant piano keyboard, and a walked into the park. Much to my surprise, in the middle of a lawn I found two street signs saying "12th St." and "Vine." An intersection that no longer existed but once had a jumping music scene was marked by an absurd signpost in the middle of nowhere, a memorial for a street corner that no longer existed, exactly on the spot where it once stood. And there was also an historical marker weathering away in the sun and rain informing us of what used to be. A city goes out of its way to create a memorial for a street corner whose fame is based on nothing but a song. I was impressed. Even the spot in Dallas where John F. Kennedy was murdered has no fancier plaque.

Kansas City has a lot of abandoned buildings, vacant homes, a lone streetcar, and an imposing World War I monument and museum. But, otherwise, there is not a lot to see. The city is famous for its delicious barbecue. Heaps of charred meat are devoured. The best joints are in the "bad" (read: Black) neighborhoods, according to the Uber drivers who don't like taking you there.

"Kansas City" has a precursor in Jim Jackson's "Kansas City Blues" from 1927.

> *If you don't want my peaches,*
>   *don't shake my tree!*
> *I ain't after that woman,*
>   *but she sure likes me*
> *I've got to move to Kansas City, mama,*
>   *sure as you're born*
> *I've got to move to Kansas City, mama,*
>   *sure as you're born*
> *I've got to move to Kansas City, honey,*
>   *where they don't 'llow you*

"Kansas City Blues"
Jim Jackson, 1927

"Kansas City" by Leiber and Stoller, originally sung by Wilbert Harrison has been covered by many: Bill Haley, The Beatles, Little Richard, Fats Domino and other lesser-known artists. So, when the wicked yet simple shuffle rhythm with its emphasis on the second and fourth beat took hold of my brain cells for good in 1976, I still had a very different "Kansas City" in my ear. Only two years earlier, the joyful Les Humphries Singers had dropped a pretty big hit of the same name:

> *Kansas City with a friend of mine*
> *We loved the women, and we had a good time*
> *Then the trouble started with a gun*
> *Then we started leaving on the run*

"Kansas City"
Les Humphries Singers, 1974

Along with St. Louis, Kansas City was once the cornerstone of the Midwest and the gateway to the vast prairie states. Kansas City's harbor was second only to Chicago's railroad station in conquering the West and was an important railroad hub, too. The Missouri-Kansas-Texas Railroad, or MKT and fondly addressed as Katy, passed through Kansas City on its way from Missouri to Texas via Kansas and Oklahoma. K.C., on the other hand, was the Kansas City Southern Railroad. By the 1920s, singers would serenade these railroad lines and Victor, one of the big record labels at the time, released both "Katy Blues" and the "K.C. Railroad Blues":

> *Katy blows this morning,*
>   *just about five miles from town*
> *Well, it blows so lonesome*
>   *all my blues are stationed down*

"Katy Blues"
Bessie Tucker, 1928

> *Thought I heard old K.C. when it blowed*
> *Blowed like it never blowed before*

"K.C. Railroad Blues"
Andrew and Jim Baxter, 1928

Bob Dylan borrowed from these songs (including their unusual past tense) when he wrote his 2012 song about the famous train from Pittsburgh, the city formerly known as Fort Duquesne:

> *Listen to that Duquesne whistle blowing*
> *Blowing like she never blowed before*

"Duquesne Whistle"
Bob Dylan, 2012

"K.C. Moan" by Son Brimmer, written for the Memphis Jug Band in 1929, leans on these same lines. It continues the implicit erotic analogy between train and woman by substituting blowing with moaning:

> *I thought I heard that K.C. when she moaned*
> *She moaned like my woman's on board*
>
> *When I get back on that K.C. road*
> *I'm going to love my baby like she's*
>   *never been loved before*

"K.C. Moan"
Son Brimmer, 1929

Trains meant freedom. That was especially true if one were behind bars. Many sang of this, such as in the songs "The Midnight Special" or "Folsom Prison Blues". Trains were often compared to or identified as women:

> *She rolled into Birmingham*
> *on a cold December day*
> *All around the station you can*
> *hear the people say*
> *She's a girl from Tennessee,*
> *she's long, boy, she's tall*
> *No changes can be taken*
> *on the Wabash Cannonball*

"The Wabash Cannonball"
traditional/Townes Van Zandt, late 19th Century/1994

"She Caught the Katy (And Left Me a Mule to Ride)" is yet another example. It was written by Taj Mahal, released in 1968, and made famous by the Blue Brothers. It refers to the Katy Train, and also clearly references "The Wabash Cannonball".

> *Well, my baby caught the Katy,*
> *she left me a mule to ride*
> *The train pulled out,*
> *and I swung on behind*
>
> *Man, my baby's long,*
> *great gosh almighty, she's tall*
> *And you know my baby's long,*
> *great gosh almighty, my baby's tall*

"She Caught the Katy (And Left Me a Mule to Ride)"
Taj Mahal, 1968

Though its great tradition is all but dead and gone, Kansas City is second only to New Orleans as a cradle of jazz. Once again, this city gets the consolation prize. Yet rhythm and blues, for instance, would be inconceivable without Kansas City, the birthplace of Wilbert Harrison and of the great blues shouter Big Joe Turner whom Elvis Presley looked up to all his life.

Turner, who was born in 1911, was a bartender in the Sunset Crystal Palace on the corner of 12th Street and Woodlawn where he met the wonderful pianist Pete Johnson and unlocked his own talent as a singer. The two formed a small band and went on to success with the song "Roll 'em, Pete" which was covered by Chuck Berry and others, some of the best representatives of the energetic piano boogie so characteristic of that time and place. Under the influence of Kansas City jazz bands, this style blossomed in postwar Texas and California evolving into rhythm and blues.

The jazz district of Kansas City, which only lives on in historic photos, was not far from the corner of 12th Street and Vine which also lives on only in memory. There are currently attempts to revive it just a few blocks away at 16th and 18th Street. That is the home of a new neighborhood, built for the Black middle class, which makes up almost a third of the population. It's not yet complete, but it is so sterile that it seems more dead than the decaying ware-houses that still dominate downtown.

But who knows? Perhaps the city will shine again with new musical contributions. In 2014, The New Basement Tapes recorded songs using unreleased lyrics written by Bob Dylan in 1967. One of the songs is about "six months in Kansas City, down on Liberty Street". Liberty Jail is a historic lockup on the outskirts of Kansas City. In 1838 and 1839, Joseph Smith, the founder of the Church of Latter-day Saints, or the Mormons, and his followers were locked up there after waging war against the state of Missouri. But

Dylan and The New Basement Tapes don't seem to have lost faith in Kansas City as fresh inspiration for songs:

> *And I love you dear, but just how long*
> *Can I keep singing the same old song?*
> *I'm going back to Kansas City*

"Kansas City"
Bob Dylan, Marcus Mumford,
& Taylor Goldsmith, 1967/2014

And that's exactly what I have in mind. I'm going back to Kansas City.

NEW ORLEANS

It all started here in this brutally hot and humid city at the mouth of the Mississippi. New Orleans is the birthplace of jazz, rock, and pop, and is one of the cities of North America most featured in song. It is a harsh place with a dark history, hard drugs, and lots of shimmering concrete. It is an urban island hugged by Lake Pontchartrain and swampland. It lies nestled behind levies that sometimes hold back the floods and sometimes do not. "N'Awlinz" is proud of its unique history and culture, which do not have much to do with the rest of the country but are still very much a part of it.

A purple, green, and gold tourism board sign when you enter New Orleans says, "Where Culture Means Business" and that's true. Tourists flock to New Orleans, the most exotic city in the nation, for entertainment and amusement. They spill out along Canal Street looking for fun at Mardi Gras, or in throng to Storyville and the old French Quarter with its wrought iron balcony railings and the heart of the city, Bourbon Street. It is second only to Las Vegas in drawing the biggest number of party-seeking Americans, but it also draws some serious jazz and blues fans. When I was first there, in 1989, I had the chance to see the guitarist Clarence Gatemouth Brown perform. It seemed that most of the audience had no idea they were listening to a legend.

Brown was very friendly and came over to talk to me at intermission. He suspected I was a colleague. During the set, he must have noticed me staring at his fingering. I did not mean to be drawing his attention, but his skill impressed me. Buddy Bolden and later Louis Armstrong were known to shroud their trumpets with a handkerchief so their competitors couldn't see exactly what or, more precisely, how they played. This is how trade secrets were protected in a city of fierce competition. But New Orleans is also a city of deep solidarity, which came especially to light after the devastation of hurricane Katrina in 2005.

Anyone who witnessed the deadly aftermath of the storm on the poverty-stricken Black community in the Lower Ninth Ward could see that even in the 21st century the US remains divided along lines of race and economic class. The Ward, which lies about six feet below sea level, like much of the city, was abandoned in its moment of need and left to fend for itself. Almost two thousand people perished because of the storm. Thousands more fled the city. Most of them were African Americans and among them were many musicians. Few returned. The Lower Ninth Ward fell into decay and remained an urban wilderness for years. Other centuries-old Black neighborhoods like Bywater were occupied by White hipsters and gentrified. The excellent TV series *Treme* (2010-13), written by David Simon and produced by HBO, gives a good perspective on this development. Dr. John, Allen Toussaint, Dave Bartholomew,

Elvis Costello, Steve Earle and many other musicians play themselves in various episodes.

New Orleans was also the starting point for many new to the continent. French explorers and pioneers ventured up the Mississippi from these docks. Others new to the continent were freshly imported slaves as New Orleans was a hub of the slave trade for a century.

> *Gold coast slave ship bound for cotton fields*
> *Sold in a market down in New Orleans*

> "Brown Sugar"
> The Rolling Stones, 1971

Enslaved people were brought to North America directly from Africa or often via the Caribbean. When Napoleon desperately needed funding for his wars and the US government feared that the French colonial power could grow too strong on its southern border, it decided to purchase the entire *Louisiane* from the Emperor of France in 1803.

Around that time criticism of slavery was growing. In 1808, the US government prohibited the import of new enslaved people, but not slavery itself. That became an enormous problem for the slave-based plantation economy of the Deep South. The plantation holders shifted to pulling from the enslaved labor pool of the more northern of the Southern states, where farming was less labor intensive. New Orleans became the center of this new, second, slave trade. It remained the most important marketplace for human lives until the Civil War. Approximately one million people were sold there, many straight from the decks of ships, but most were marketed from slave pens. Until 1829, these slave pens were in the French Quarter. A few historical marker plaques on old walls between the bars and clubs are reminders of these dark stains on America's history. Later the refined aristocratic citizens relegated slave pens and auction blocks to less visible areas on the outskirts of town. Today just two of the 52 documented slave auction houses are memorialized with historical plaques. Slaves were auctioned like used cars and often sold again and again. The auction blocks were the absolute epitome of humiliation and degradation, and each sale was a step toward an uncertain future as the property of a new owner.

Louisiana slavery was not just confined to the agricultural and plantation economies. It was also part of the operations of the port of New Orleans itself. The main center of the slave trade relied itself on many slaves. It was unique because no other city in the country had slaves in it, other than small numbers of house slaves. The slaves in New Orleans had unique privileges. The enslaved, who were mostly French Creole speaking, were allowed to use tools and horses and work in skilled trades. As a result, they developed self-confidence. Many of them were allowed to have personal property and were able to partially purchase their freedom with it.

> *No more auction block for me*
> *No more, no more*
> *No more auction block for me*
> *Many thousands gone*

"No More Auction Block"
traditional, approx. 1865

After the Louisiana Purchase, which included New Orleans, Napoleon played a decisive role for a second time in the history of the city at the mouth of the Mississippi. His battles with the British had significant consequences for the new nation. Because America traded with France and parts of Europe occupied by Great Britain, the British blockaded America's harbors to deter this trade and weaken Napoleon. Britain did not back down to US demands, there were skirmishes and in 1812 war broke out.

In New Orleans the war led to a bizarre, but important chapter in the development of the United States. In December 1814, seasoned British soldiers were shipped to Louisiana and in January 1815 they were defeated by a vastly outnumbered ragtag American army, a hodgepodge of mercenaries from Haiti, citizens of New Orleans, and some pirates and Choctaw Indians lead by General Andrew Jackson, who later became the President of the United States:

> *In 1814 we took a little trip*
> *Along with Colonel Jackson down the mighty Mississippi*
> *And we caught the bloody British in the*
> *town of New Orleans*
>
> *We fired our guns, and the British kept a-comin'*
> *There wasn't as many as there was a while ago*
> *We fired once more, and they began to runnin'*
> *On down the Mississippi to the Gulf of Mexico*

"The Battle of New Orleans"
Jimmy Driftwood, 1959

The macabre historical irony was that neither side knew that two weeks earlier the Treaty of Ghent had been signed by the British envoy and future President John Quincy

Adams. The war was already over. This delay in communications cost 2,700 Britons and 71 American lives.

With its history of change and multicultural population, New Orleans became not only the cradle of jazz, but also more diverse than the rest of the USA. It was a true melting pot. On the one hand, creolization created the city's distinct fusion sound, but on the other hand made an opening for improvisation. As a result, New Orleans became the undisputed and most important Mecca of American music.

Buddy Bolden, who was memorialized by Michael Ondaatje in the novel *Buddy Bolden's Blues* (1995) and in the equally beautiful song of the same name by Jelly Roll Morton in 1939, Louis Armstrong, Professor Longhair, Irma Thomas, Champion Jack Dupree, Huey Smith, Mahalia Jackson, Fats Domino, Dave Bartholomew, Dr. John, the Neville Brothers, Alan Toussaint, the Preservation Hall Jazz Band, the Dirty Dozen Brass Band, Randy Newman, Wynton and Branford Marsalis—these are just some of the famous jazz and pop musicians the city bred. And don't forget Little Richard, from Macon, Georgia, but recorded his rock 'n' roll hits in New Orleans. It also drew numerous Cajun and Zydeco musicians from the bayous surrounding New Orleans. And it was a magnet for musicians like Willy de Ville and Leon Russell, who were clearly influenced by the NOLA nasal vocal style, relentless triplets on the piano, or the Second Line drumming, even though they were not from New Orleans.

The Second Line is a key descriptor for the music from New Orleans. It is an immediately recognizable rhythm, but it is hard to explain. In the '90s, I coincidentally heard a show on NPR in New Haven, Connecticut, where Dr. John explained it well. According to Mac Rebennack, aka Dr. John, there are basically two ways of playing percussion: *definado*, i.e., precisely on the beat in 4/4 time, or *indefinado*, playfully around the beat on 2 and 4 (in New Orleans also like a march on beat 1 and 3), always prancing, varying, building and reducing tension. That is the principle of the Second Line.

The term itself comes from the brass bands that accompany processions of the dead to their burials in the cemeteries of Catholic New Orleans. Traditionally, they play a slow, slow tempo to mourning melodies on the way there and after the funeral on the way back they pick up the tempo with exuberant happiness. Of course, the marching band has its own drummers. But they are joined by people from the neighborhood. Children get in on the action and run back and forth. They have percussion instruments, drums, rattles, tambourines, and they fill the space between the four beats on the four quarters that the band specifies. Out of respect they keep their distance from the parade. They form the second line. The rhythm rolls, varies and is incredibly laid back.

Dr. John said it like this: "When we have funerals in New Orleans, the people marchin' in respect to the graveyard—that is the second line. When they put the body down and the band strikes up a lively tune to bring the people home, the dance the people are doing behind the band—that is also the second line. The people that follow the funeral is the second line. It grew to mean the people that follow the parade, the band that follows the float. But when we put people down, we have a good time about it."

In the last few years, New Orleans lost most of the musicians who shaped its music for decades, artists who stood as international figureheads for the creativity and energy of the city: in 2015 the outstanding producer Allen Toussaint, Ellis Marsalis, the patriarch of a whole family of jazz wunderkinds (Branford, Wynton, Delfeayo, and Jason) in 2020, Fats Domino in 2017, and in June 2019 his musically indispensable companion, the great composer, arranger and trumpeter Dave Bartholomew. Also in June 2019, the most important New Orleans musician of two entire generations died: Dr. John. He was the mastermind of the New Orleans music scene and the direct heir of Professor Longhair (aka Henry Roeland Byrd), in the prestigious line of Jelly Roll Morton as the city's chief pianist. At the news of Dr. John's death, a second line that stretched ten blocks formed spontaneously. The police did not understand what was happening. Dr. John was a high priest of the musical and spiritual identity of New Orleans, keeper of tradition and radical innovator at the same time.

> *Way down yonder on the farm*
> *We go ballin' with Dr. John*

"Down Yonder We Go Ballin'"
Smiley Lewis, 1956

He recorded versions of "Tipitina", Professor Longhair's greatest hit. Dr. John's version can hardly be distinguished from the original. But he has also recorded funk and jazz numbers, sometimes with a large orchestra, made film music and played with all the great names in rock music. He started as a guitarist until someone shot his left ring finger away. Apart from Django Reinhardt, no guitarist has been able to cope with the loss of that finger, and so Dr. John switched to bass (although a complete fingering hand is also an advantage here) before he finally settled on piano.

Dr. John grew up not only with music, but also around prostitution, violence, and drugs. He dealt the latter but was also one of his own best customers. After some time behind bars in Fort Worth, Texas, he emigrated to Los Angeles in 1965. From there he found much more fame than he did in New Orleans, perhaps driven by homesickness for his city:

> *Do you know what it means to miss New Orleans*
> *And miss her each night and day?*

> "Do You Know What It Means to Miss New Orleans?"
> DeLange/Alter for Armstrong/Holiday, 1947

Antoine Dominique Domino Jr. longed so much for the city of his 1928 birth that he said he would return there on foot if necessary:

> *I'm going to need two pair of shoes*
> *When I get through walkin' these blues*
> *When I get back to New Orleans*
>
> *I'm leavin' here today*
> *Yes, I'm goin' back home to stay*
> *Yes, I'm walkin' to New Orleans*

> "Walking To New Orleans"
> Bobby Charles for Fats Domino, 1960

Fats Domino recorded his first song in 1949. Strictly speaking, "The Fat Man" was not his song, because Champion Jack Dupree, also born in New Orleans, but in 1909, had already recorded it as "Junker Blues" in 1940 with comparatively moderate success. Domino only changed the tempo a little bit, but he radically altered the text. Dupree's song was an unapologetic pro-drug number:

> *Some people call me a junker,*
> *'cause I'm loaded all the time*
>
> *Some people say I use a needle,*
> *and some say I slip cocaine*
>
> *I just want my reefer,*
> *I just want to feel high again*

"Junker Blues"
Champion Jack Dupree, 1940

This debauchery did not go over well with a larger, White audience, of course. Louis Armstrong showed he could be successful with a White audience by playing the stereotype of a good-natured, slightly stupid, and always cheerful "Negro," as it was called back then, a kind of Uncle Tom. White singers, such as Bill Haley, have smoothed out clearly ambiguous lyrics by Black singers like Big Joe Turner to avoid any moral offense. For example, in Turner's original "Shake, Rattle and Roll" he sang:

> *You're wearin' those dresses that*
> *the sun comes shining through*
> *I can't believe my eyes*
> *all this belongs to you*
>
> *I'm like a one-eyed cat peepin'*
> *in a seafood store*

> *Well, I can look at you and tell*
> *you ain't no child no more…*

"Shake, Rattle and Roll"
Big Joe Turner, 1954

Bill Haley found those lines improper for his young White audience. He had a huge hit in 1954 with the following mangled version of the song:

> *You're wearin' those dresses,*
> *your hair done up so nice*
> *You look so warm,*
> *but your heart is cold as ice*
>
> *I'm like a one-eyed cat, peepin'*
> *in a seafood store*
> *I can look at you and tell*
> *you don't love me no more*

"Shake, Rattle and Roll"
Bill Haley's Version,
also 1954

Fats Domino also chose those two strategies. In his version, temptation is resisted but he is allowed a greedy look at the Creole mulatto girls:

> *But the girls they love me,*
> *'cause I know my way around […]*
>
> *I was watchin', watchin', watchin'*
> *all these Creole gals […]*
>
> *'Cause women and a bad life,*

they're carrying this soul away [...]

"The Fat Man"
Domino/Bartholomew, 1949

That allowed Fats Domino to find success with a White audience. "The Fat Man" was his breakthrough song. He was beloved his entire life primarily by White fans, especially in Europe. Champion Jack Dupree had a similar, albeit less happy experience. He moved to Europe in the 1960s and died in Hanover, Germany, in 1992.

Dr. John, however, driven by his longing for New Orleans, moved back home:

> *I'm goin' back to home to my baby*
> *Goin' back to New Orleans*
>
> *Want to plant my feet on Rampart Street*
> *Be there for the Mardi Gras*
>
> *And never more will I roam*
> *Goin' get me a fill of that étouffée*
> *'Cause New Orleans is my home*

"Goin' Back to New Orleans"
Joe Liggins and The Honeydrippers, 1989

Mardi Gras in New Orleans is a huge tourist draw. But it has an influence on the city's culture that goes far beyond its economic impact. To understand these traditions, it is important to know a few words: *Mardi Gras* translated from the French means Fat Tuesday. It is the climax of carnival festivities brought to Southern Louisiana by the Catholic French. There are numerous krewes or clubs, like samba schools in Rio de Janeiro. They have evocative names like Mistick Krewe of Comus or Rex, the Knights of Momus or Zulu Social Aid & Pleasure Club led by a Zulu King or Queen. The crowd erupts into ecstasy at the sight of them.

> *Well, I'm goin' to New Orleans*
> *I wanna see the Mardi Gras*
>
> *When I get to New Orleans*
> *I wanna see the Zulu King*
>
> *Gonna make it my standin' place*
> *Until I see the Zulu Queen*

> "Mardi Gras In New Orleans"
> Professor Longhair, 1949

The krewes play an important part in strengthening and stabilizing the African American population of New Orleans. Members wave flags with their krewe colors like those of a sports team and egg each other on. The song "Iko, Iko", made famous in the Dr. John version of 1972, speaks to this.

> *Jock-a-mo fee-no ai na-né,*
> *jock-a-mo fee na-né*
>
> *My flag boy and your flag boy*
> *were sittin' by the fire.*
> *My flag boy told your flag boy:*
> *"I'm gonna set your flag on fire."*

> "Iko, Iko" (e.g.: Chock-A-Mo),
> James Sugar Boy Crawford, 1953

Dr. John, the Night Tripper, was an initiated voodoo priest ("I been hoo-doo'd"). He was raised with dark fantasies and visions of death, bizarre rituals, sacrificial offerings, and hypnotic sorcery. These rituals played a significant role in the Creole syncretistic culture of New Orleans. Today much of this is no longer understood.

What do these lyrics mean? The flag boy story is straightforward enough. Just like rival college sports fans try to steal or deface each other's mascots, the flag boys of the different krewes set the flags of their competition on fire before Mardi Gras.

But not one person today listening to this very popular song knows what "jock-a-mo fee na-né" means. Though everyone sings along. It's probably not a remnant of French from the city's past. Experts debate if it is a fragment of an indigenous or West African language. Regardless, this shows how New Orleans clings to its musical traditions and how casually everything here is combined in one stew pot to create a spicy musical gumbo or jambalaya, where the elements are still recognizable. These are, historically, slave foods, like Brazilian feijoada, with the addition of seafood and fish provided by the sea, swamps, lakes, and big river. Musical gumbo describes the syncretistic fusion that occurred here as well. The mix included French nobility, landowners and slave traders, Anglophone and European settlers, Hispanics, and dozens of very different Native American peoples, slaves from West Africa, slaves from the Caribbean and francophone Cajuns. These migrants who were driven out of Canada in the 18th century, were not warmly welcomed by the established French-speaking residents of New Orleans and therefore settled in the swamps and bayous.

The term "Creole" is not pejorative or insulting and describes not only this mix, but also the offspring of French and Spanish immigrants. Originally, it was used to differentiate between those born in Europe and those born in the New World. In New Orleans, Creoles are descendants of African as well as early French and Caribbean settlers. And, unlike in other places, this established group is highly respected.

> *There's a man in New Orleans*
> *Who plays rock 'n' roll*
> *He's a guitar man*
> *With a great big soul*
> *He goes by the name of "King Creole"*

When the King starts playing his guitar, bending the strings, and singing, growling "from way down his throat", everybody is in awe.

> *Well, he sings a song about a crawdad hole*
> *He sings a song about a jelly roll*
> *He sings a song about meat and greens*
> *He sings some blues about New Orleans*

"King Creole"
Leiber/Stoller for Elvis Presley, 1958

It's this Creole and francophone cultural history that makes New Orleans an exotic playground for Americans. New Orleans is one of the most exotic destinations an American can visit without a passport or the risk of foreign travel. Caribbean and European influences converge to create an exciting, yet easily consumed Creole mélange. It evokes illicit fantasies, but without risk, like a peepshow. New Orleans is looked down upon, but it is also glamorized. It has long been the subject of clichés and many myths about the city are firmly held. Back In 1922, "Way Down Yonder in New Orleans" was written as part of a musical revue on Broadway. The song describes New Orleans as an exotic, erotic paradise, long before drugs and music itself became the themes of the music from and about the city. This kind of stereotyping remained unchanged over the next hundred years. Women are represented in the traditional folklore of New Orleans only as "Creole babies," prostitutes, or gypsy fortunetellers:

> *Well, way down yonder in New Orleans*
> *in the land of the dreamy scenes*
> *There's a Garden of Eden,*
> *you know what I mean*
>
> *Creole babies with flashin' eyes*
> *softly whisper with tender sighs*
> *And then you stop*
> *You bet your life you'll linger there a little while*
>
> *There is heaven right here on earth*
> *with those beautiful queens*
> *Way down yonder*
> *in New Orleans*

"Way Down Yonder in New Orleans"
Layton/Creamer, 1922

The rock 'n' roll singer Freddy Cannon had his biggest hit with a version of "Way Down Yonder in New Orleans" in 1959.

But, of course, the music *from* New Orleans is even more interesting than the music *about* New Orleans. Louis Armstrong was its greatest ambassador. In 1928, he sang Spencer Williams's "Basin Street Blues". Williams was born in 1889 in New Orleans and literally grew up in a brothel. Armstrong was also born in New Orleans, in 1901, and spent most of his childhood in an orphanage called the Colored Waif's Home for Boys. When "Basin Street Blues" was written in 1928, the houses of ill repute that once lined Basin Street were long gone.

> *Won't you come along with me*
> *Down the Mississippi?*
> *We'll take a boat to the land of dreams*
> *Come along with me on down to New Orleans!*
>
> *Now the band's there to greet us*
> *Old friends will meet us*
> *Heaven on earth. They call it Basin Street*
>
> *New Orleans, land of dreams*

"Basin Street Blues"
Spencer Williams, 1928

New Orleans as the American capital of sin and vice was always a favorite motif in popular music, literature, and film. And that certainly was not without basis. The old folk song "House of the Rising Sun" is probably the most famous song ever about a brothel. It was a huge hit for The Animals in 1964 and had been very explicit in its warning, albeit a bit theatrical, since 1933, concerning the consequences of a life of sin. In the traditional version, a poor girl sings the touching story of her life. Eric Burdon, front man for The Animals, was forced to make a poor boy out of her and it robs the text of some of its morality tale qualities:

> *There is a house in New Orleans*
> *They call "The Rising Sun"*
> *And it's been the ruin of many a poor boy*
> *And God I know I'm one*
>
> *Oh mother tell your children*
> *Not to do what I have done*
> *Spend your life in sin and misery*
> *In the House of the Rising Sun!*
>
> *I'm goin' back to New Orleans*
> *To wear that ball and chain*

"House of the Rising Sun"
Traditional/The Animals, 17th Century/1964

However, most of the songs about New Orleans are not cautionary tales about straying from the straight and narrow, but rather more hedonistic calls to wanton excess. The food and drink flow heavy and rich in the Crescent City.

Stick McGhee recorded his biggest hit, a song about excessive drinking, in 1949: "Drinkin' Wine Spoo-Dee-O-Dee". It's been covered many times and Jerry Lee Lewis laid down the best-known version, its lyrics showcasing an idealized description of the rock 'n' roll lifestyle:

> *Down in New Orleans, where everything's fine*
> *All them cats are drinkin' that wine*
> *Drinkin' that mess is their delight*
> *When they get drunk start singin' all night...*

> *"Drinkin' wine spo-dee-o-dee*
> *Pass that bottle to me!"*

"Drinkin' Wine Spo-dee-o-dee"
Stick McGhee, 1949

The praises, musically, heaped upon the city at the mouth of the Mississippi and especially on Basin, Dumaine and, most of all, Rampart Streets are nearly endless. One more song, "The Mojo Boogie" by the still underestimated J.B. Lenoir in 1965, brings it full circle:

> *I been to New Orleans*
>   *and I sure had a wonderful time*
> *I was high,*
>   *high as a Georgia pine*
>
> *My auntie carried me all down*
>   *on Rampart Street*
>
> *Seen everybody*
>   *I wanted to meet*
>
> *Got that Mojo Boogie,*
>   *begin to slide on down*
>
> *They got the Louisiana boogie,*
>
> *They even got the thing they*
>   *call the mojo hand*

"The Mojo Boogie"
J.B. Lenoir, 1965

What is a mojo hand anyway? It is what White people call the Native American "medicine:" a sack filled with various herbs and small symbolic items to deflect evil magic and to magically attract women. Even more powerful than amulets in old Europe, the mojo hand is a very important voodoo cult object that not only serves to passively protect, but also actively aid in life's situations. The term "hand" could perhaps be a reference to Fatima's Hand, which is well known in North and Western Africa where most slaves taken to America came from and is said to protect against the evil eye. The mojo hand is sometimes called a "gris-gris", which is also the name of Dr. John's first album. And of course, every blues fan knows "mojo hand" from Muddy Waters' "Got My Mojo Workin'":

> *Going down to Louisiana to get me a mojo hand*
> *I'm gonna have all you women under my command*
>
> *I got a gypsy woman givin' me advice*
> *I got a whole lotta tricks keepin' her at night*
>
> "Got My Mojo Working"
Preston Foster, 1956

Of course, a real mojo hand can only be gotten from a gypsy down in Louisiana or from your local, trusted voodoo priest. It is worth the trip, though. Especially for the music. I'm going back to New Orleans.

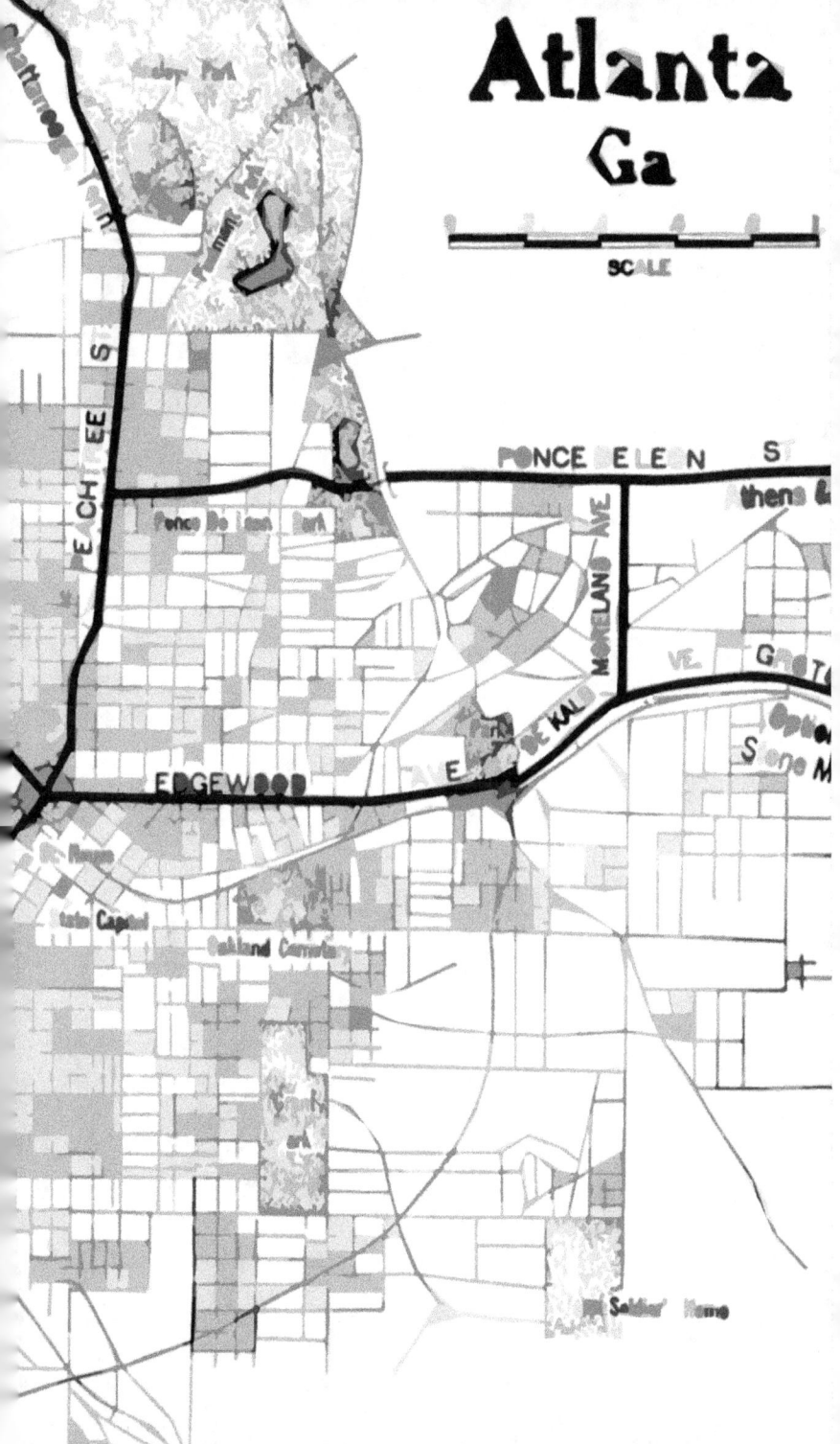

ATLANTA

New Orleans rightfully claims to be the birthplace of jazz and pop music. But the second most important city in the South for the development of the music culture and business of the 1920s was clearly Atlanta, Georgia. Most importantly, Atlanta was one of the first centers of the developing record industry, long before Los Angeles, Memphis or Nashville.

Atlanta rose to importance because it was the final stop on an important rail line from the North. That gave the small town the descriptive name of "Terminus," end of the line. It was renamed in 1845 to Atlanta, probably after the Western & Atlantic Railroad. The town had just nine thousand inhabitants at the beginning of the Civil War in 1861, but it was of the highest strategic importance because it had become the central railroad hub of the South. The fact that Atlanta could be reached easily from every city of the Confederate states was its death sentence. Union General George Stoneman repeatedly tore up the Richmond and Danville Railroad, the steel artery that connected Richmond, capital of the Confederates, with the other Southern states, essential for the survival of the Confederation. This led to insurmountable supply issues and famine. Richmond finally fell in 1865.

> *Virgil Caine is my name,*
>   *and I served on the Danville train*
> *'Till Stoneman's cavalry came*
>   *and tore up the tracks again*
> *In the winter of '65 we were hungry,*
>   *just barely alive*
> *By May, the tenth, Richmond had fell,*
>   *it was a time I remember oh so well*
> *The night they drove old Dixie down,*
>   *and the bells were ringing...*

"The Night They Drove Old Dixie Down"
Robbie Robertson, 1969

Jefferson Davis, the Confederate President, fleeing with his entire cabinet, pulled out of Richmond on a train of the Richmond and Danville Railroad that had been patched up once again, and desperately attempted to govern from Danville. But once the Union troops destroyed the railroad tracks again, the Confederate forces could no longer be supplied. Their commander, Robert E. Lee, had to abandon the tracks for good while William Tecumseh Sherman's Union troops took Atlanta after a long siege and burned it down to its foundations. Roughly seventy thousand soldiers perished in the battles for Atlanta. The Confederacy finally capitulated on April 9, 1865.

Although Atlanta quickly rebuilt after the war and has long been a confident and successful commercial center, the capital of Georgia suffers to this day from a bit of posttraumatic syndrome. Bookshops are full of newly released titles on the "War of Northern Aggression," as the Confederate patriots used to call it, as if they are still trying to win that war. In the late 1980s when I lived in Atlanta, I made a big impression there with my still fresh university knowledge of American history. It opened doors for me, for example, to know a few things about Stonewall Jackson and to be able to understand the Southern Drawl. There's a Southern accent even where I come from, too—Bavaria!

Atlanta remains a transportation hub, despite the decline in rail travel. The road west, to the Promised Land, still goes through Atlanta, though, be it for planes, cars or the Greyhound bus:

> *I left my home in Norfolk Virginia*
> *California on my mind*
> *Straddled that Greyhound and rode him into Raleigh*
> *And on across Caroline*
> *We stopped in Charlotte, bypassed Rock Hill*
> *We never was a minute late*
> *We was ninety miles out of Atlanta by sundown*
> *Rolling out of Georgia state*

"Promised Land"
Chuck Berry, 1964

Perhaps as a reaction to its defeat in the Civil War, Southerners tended to glorify their long-gone aristocratic way of life. Plantations with enormous fields of sugar, cotton and tobacco once dominated the South. The feudalistic system continued until long after the war. Earlier, of course, there were slaves and but a small caste of skilled workers like blacksmiths and printers. But there was a very affluent, spoiled upper class of land owners. The South had been under the flags of Spain and France until not long before and due to its Spanish and French heritage, the Southern upper class embraced the rich Romanic culture which in their case had become a largely hollow façade. This did not sit well with the poor White tenant farmers or sharecroppers, who were in turn called "clay-eaters" or "crackers" by the city dwellers. The soft, effeminate manners of the landed gentry, who were left behind by history with their perfumed handkerchiefs and gold-handled canes, were subject to both secret admiration and deep disdain. If you have ever seen *Gone with the Wind* or the late singer Willy DeVille, you will recognize the type.

The Civil War brought a sudden end to the world of country gentlemen and their southern belles in their mansions and plantation homes. But now this allegedly glorious past was all the more idealized and stubbornly mystified. The South became the *imagined* South, a world smelling of magnolias and bourbon. It was peopled by beaus with heavy rings on their fingers extravagantly dressed in old-fashioned frocks and ruffled shirts, holding their mint juleps on the veranda. Even if you disregard these characters of the vanished Old South, its atmosphere has since been informed by a melancholic longing for the lost homeland.

> *The distant moanin' of a train*
> *Seems to play a sad refrain to the night*
> *A rainy night in Georgia*
> *A rainy night in Georgia*
> *I believe it's rainin' all over the world*

"Rainy Night in Georgia"
Tony Joe White, 1967

Hoagy Carmichael's wonderful love song "Georgia on

My Mind" became a global hit in Ray Charles's 1960 recording. Charles was born in Albany, Georgia, in 1930, the year the song was written. In 1979, it became the official anthem of the State of Georgia. However, from the very start it was disputed whether the song idealized the state or a woman of the same name:

> *Georgia, Georgia!*
> *The whole day through*
> *Just an old sweet song*
> *Keeps Georgia on my mind*
>
> *I said Georgia, Georgia!*
> *A song of you*
> *Comes as sweet and clear*
> *As moonlight through the pines*
>
> *Other arms reach out to me*
> *Other eyes smile tenderly*
> *Still in the peaceful dreams I see*
> *The road leads back to you*
>
> *I said, Georgia, oh Georgia!*
> *No peace I find*
> *Just an old sweet song*
> *Keeps Georgia on my mind*

"Georgia on My Mind"
Hoagy Carmichael, 1930

So, what is this song about? Do the good people of Georgia fall into the same trap as Chicagoans who made "Sweet Home Chicago" their anthem although that song is, without doubt, about Port Chicago in California? The lyrics are fairly clear:

> *Other arms reach out to me*
> *Other eyes smile tenderly*

These lines could only be written about a human being named Georgia. The song must really be about a woman. And, as everybody knows, Hoagy Carmichael's sister was named Georgia.

But isn't that the wrong question? Isn't there an age-old tradition of referring to countries as female and personifying them allegorically as women? Once the praised homeland itself is eroticized, the object of the praise becomes potentially metaphorical, and it doesn't matter if the song is about a woman or a place.

But the South has a different meaning for Whites than for African Americans. It is not hard to understand that in the face of the heritage of slavery, the Ku Klux Klan, and frequent lynching, Black Americans are not as enthusiastic as some Whites about the glorification of the past (as, for example, in election slogans like "Make America Great Again").

> *Southern trees bear strange fruit*
> *Blood on the leaves and blood at the root*
> *Black bodies swinging in the Southern breeze*
> *Strange fruit hanging from the poplar trees*
>
> *Pastoral scene of the gallant South*
> *The bulging eyes and the twisted mouth*
> *Scent of magnolias, sweet and fresh*
> *Then the sudden smell of burning flesh*
>
> *Here is fruit for the crows to pluck*
> *For the rain to gather, for the wind to suck*
> *For the sun to rot, for the trees to drop*

Here is a strange and bitter crop

"Strange Fruit"
Abel Meeropol, 1939

Southern life was not pleasant for everyone. The gallant South is continually called to reckon with its past. Often this is not of its own accord but driven by liberal Yankee intellectuals from the North. Randy Newman beautifully highlights this with his unique, biting, yet elegant sarcasm. He introduces his song "Rednecks" like this:

> *Last night I saw Lester Maddox on TV*
> *With some smart-ass New York Jew*
> *And the Jew laughed at Lester Maddox*
> *And the audience laughed at Lester Maddox, too*

Lester Maddox was the governor of Georgia from 1966 to 1970. Born in Atlanta in 1915, he lived there as a convinced and vocal proponent of segregation until he died in 2003. After his brief preamble, Newman slips into the role of a Southern redneck defender:

> *We got no-necked oilmen from Texas*
> *And good ol' boys from Tennessee*
> *And college men from LSU*
> *Went in dumb, come out dumb, too*
> *Hustlin' 'round Atlanta in their alligator shoes*
> *Gettin' drunk every weekend at the barbecue*
> *And they're keepin' the niggers down*

"Rednecks"
Randy Newman, 1974

In the minds of some, a southern accent and drinking are

the first things that come to mind when northern smart-asses think about Southerners.

> *There's a Southern accent where I come from*
> *The young'uns call it "country"*
> *The Yankees call it dumb [...]*
>
> *I got my own way of talkin'*
> *But everything is done with a Southern accent*
> *Where I come from*

"Southern Accents"
Tom Petty, 1985

In Randy Newman's college men from LSU (Louisiana State University), "hustlin' 'round Atlanta in their alligator shoes," these slick, no-good, ne'er-do-well dandies are a caricature of the cultivated, refined Rhett Butler from *Gone with the Wind*. These figures are cut of the same cloth as those mentioned in Bob Dylan's "Blind Willie McTell", his epic homage to the great blues guitar player and singer from Georgia. In just four lines he perfectly summarizes this character's glitz and decadence:

> *There's a woman by the river*
> *With some fine young, handsome man*
> *He's dressed up like a squire*
> *Bootlegged whiskey in his hand*

"Blind Willie McTell"
Bob Dylan, 1983

Looking like gentry, but with cheap moonshine in his hand: this is what had become of the once grandiose cavaliers of the South. This is how similar they have become to rednecks, the poor White riffraff from the back country, now that the abolishment of slavery has taken away both their fortunes and feudalistic way of life. They have become nothing but shadows from a world vanished long ago.

The redneck, however, is alive. In Georgia the redneck is, by definition, a daredevil—literally. He can take on the devil himself, like Charlie Daniels, one of the conservative representatives of Southern Rock, told us in "The Devil Went down to Georgia":

> *The Devil went down to Georgia,*
> *He was looking for a soul to steal*
> *He was in a bind, 'cause he was way behind,*
> *He was willing to make a deal*

"The Devil Went down to Georgia"
Charlie Daniels Band, 1979

The devil is unaware of what this fearless young man can do and challenges Johnny to a fiddling contest. And so, it begins:

> *Johnny, rosin up your bow and play your fiddle hard*
> *'Cause hell's broke loose in Georgia,*
> *and the devil deals the cards*

And the story continues:

> *Fire on the mountain, run, boys, run!*
> *The devil's in the House of the Rising Sun*
> *Chicken in the bread pan picking out dough*
> *Granny, does your dog bite? "No, child, no"*
>
> *The Devil bowed his head, because he knew*
> *that he'd been beat*

*And he laid that golden fiddle on the ground
at Johnny's feet*

It is no coincidence that Daniels tells the tale of a fiddler from Georgia who bests the devil. Fiddlin' John Carson, the first fiddler of the Country and Hillbilly genres, came from Georgia, too.

Just like the devil who went down to Georgia, many Appalachians moved south in the 1920s. Like most of them, Carson first worked in the cotton mills. The impoverished hillbillies from the Blue Ridge Mountains or from the Ozarks moved to Atlanta for the jobs in the textile industry. Before it became a demeaning insult "hillbilly" referred to Protestant refugees from Scotland or Ireland who were loyal to William of Orange. They came to the US and had little choice but to settle in the most infertile and inhospitable parts of the Appalachian Mountains. Clay eaters, of course, were people so poor they literally ate clay and usually contracted hook worm and, as a consequence, anemia, depression, apathy, and an early death. But in 1923, Carson, the devilishly good musician, recorded his first disc.

During the Great Migration, millions of Blacks from the Cotton Belt of the South relocated to the Rust Belt of the North with its steel mills and car factories. Just as African Americans took country blues from the Mississippi Delta to Chicago, the hillbillies and clay eaters carried a rich musical tradition of Scottish, Irish and English ballads with their modest baggage when they migrated South instead of in the opposite direction. They also brought their fiddles. It was this migration that laid the cornerstone of what became country music. It also made Atlanta, long before Nashville, a musical Mecca and one of the most important places for the nation's recording industry. Business boomed for Atlanta's record companies between 1920 and 1950. Ragtime and blues were also recorded.

From early on there were songs about Atlanta and Georgia, like Cow Cow Davenport's "Atlanta Rag" from 1929 or Henry Williams & Eddie Anthony's "Georgia Crawl" from the prior year. The African American Eddie Anthony was also a fiddler. Even ragtime numbers were fiddled then:

> *Come here papa, look at sis*
> *Out in the backyard just shaking like this*
> *Doin' the Georgia Crawl, oh Georgia Crawl*
> *You don't need to buy a thing, do the Georgia Crawl*
>
> *I can shake it east, shake it west*
> *Way down south I can shake it the best*
>
> *Come in this house, gal, come here right now*
> *Out there trying to do the crawl*
>   *and you don't know how!*
>
> *Old aunt Sally, old and gray*
> *Doin' the Georgia Crawl till she died away*
> *Doin' the Georgia Crawl, oh Georgia Crawl*
> *You don't need to buy a thing, do the Georgia Crawl*

"Georgia Crawl"
Henry Williams & Eddie Anthony, 1928

Trixie Smith (1895-1943), Big Maceo Merriweather (1905-1953), Gladys Knight, and Brenda Lee were all from Atlanta. And one of the most important Southern Rock Bands ever was the Allman Brothers Band from Macon, Georgia, which is also the home of Little Richard. The Allman Brothers Band dedicated their instrumental "Hot 'Lanta" to the city of Atlanta. The song was released in

1971 and became the signature tune of the band's bassist Berry Oakley. He died in a bizarre motorcycle accident. The accident itself was not really bizarre. It was the fact that 24-year-old Duane Allman, the band's guitarist, had died a year earlier at nearly the same place, also on a motorbike.

Southern rock seems to be unhealthy in a different way from rock music in general. Its representatives don't die at twenty-seven of overdoses as is customary for rock stars. Instead, they die in crashes. Lynyrd Skynyrd, the other great band from the South hailed from Jacksonville, Florida. Three band members were killed, and the others were badly injured when their plane went down in Mississippi. Buddy Holly from Lubbock, Texas, was in a plane that went down in 1959 together with Richie Valens and the Big Bopper. And in 1990 the guitar legend Stevie Ray Vaughn from Dallas, Texas, died in a helicopter accident. The Allman Brothers Band, however, perished on a road in Georgia.

> *Georgia, Georgia [...]*
> *The road leads back to you...*

BIRMINGHAM AND ALABAMA

The exploitation of slaves on cotton and sugar plantations as it still existed in the first half of the 19th century was abolished because of the Civil War. Slavery as an economic system was no longer profitable due to accelerating industrialization. It became clear it was cheaper to hire poorly paid workers than to hold slaves because slave-owners had to protect and support the lives of those slaves, their workforce, their investments. This was purely in their own best selfish economic interest, not at all driven by a humane motive. With paid labor, however, those expenses were not on their dime. And then there were new machines which promised returns on their investment that were even more lucrative than either slaves or impoverished laborers.

This did not ease the suppression of African American populations in the South though. "That peculiar institution," as slavery was often euphemistically referred to, had been replaced by other instruments of oppression a hundred years later, namely the penitentiary system and forced labor. This shifts our focus from the lands of traditional, pseudo-feudal plantations of the 18th and 19th century, like in Louisiana and Georgia, to the huge penitentiary farms in Mississippi and Alabama. They still exist today. Although it was only until the middle of the 20th century that they were of any economic import. But that is the time we are most interested in for musical reasons. Let's first turn our attention to the state of Alabama.

Alabama is an exhausted place, putrid and humid. It is weary to the bone after centuries of hard labor, hatred, violence and poverty, the highest poverty rate in the US. For example, Jefferson County, with its county seat of Birmingham, had to file for bankruptcy in 2011. Debts of over three billion dollars burdened a county of just 660,000 inhabitants. The main reason was bad investments in the privatization of the wastewater treatment facility. Water and sewer bills had quadrupled. In Butler County, however, sewage continues to flow freely into open ditches. In 2017, there were still hook worm epidemics in Alabama like those otherwise seen only in the poorest countries in the world. "This land is your land," sang Woody Guthrie; "This land is condemned," sang Bob Dylan in contrast. The history of Alabama is the history of violence against the weak, justified by racism. Montgomery is now home to a memorial for the more than four thousand known victims of racist lynchings in the South.

Birmingham is the largest city in Alabama. Another town had been founded in 1813 in the same place on Choctaw land. Then iron ore was discovered. The first steel mill was erected in 1861. When Birmingham was founded ten years later it was named after the English center of the steel industry. Thousands of workers moved there. Mining and steel production flourished. In the thirty years until 1910 the population of Birmingham soared from three thousand to a hundred and thirty thousand. But as quickly as the number of jobs and inhabitants had grown, they crashed. The world market stagnated in the 1960s. The quality of the ore could not compete nor could labor costs. By now most of the jobs are long gone. They went to countries in which the wages and production costs are lower.

> *They complained in the East, they are paying too high*
> *They say that your ore ain't worth digging*
> *That it's much cheaper down in the South American*
>   *towns*
> *Where the miners work almost for nothing*

"North Country Blues"
Bob Dylan, 1964

Between 1950 and 2000, the number of those employed in the Birmingham steel industry fell from about thirty thousand to roughly a thousand. And because there are no other industries, unemployment remains persistent for the majority of Alabama's former steel workers, most of whom are African American. Almost forty percent of the population of Selma lives below the poverty line, and nearly all of the poorest are African American. In spite of Selma, Birmingham, Montgomery, and Mobile, Alabama is mostly agrarian and rural. Even now, as in the days of slavery on the large plantations, cotton, sugar, and tobacco grows from the heavy, black soil.

Ma Rainey, presumably the greatest female blues vocalist of all time, was probably born in 1882 in Russell County, Alabama, as Gertrude Pridgett. The vast majority of the population of that area descended from enslaved people. There was a paper-thin layer of White upper class, but they lacked the sophistication found in similar groups in Georgia or Louisiana. And then there were the sharecroppers, White crackers, and clay eaters, impoverished and reactionary. This is the group that was and is systematically manipulated by wealthy Whites and their politicians. They have often been weaponized against African Americans:

> *A South politician preaches to the poor white man*
> *"You got more than the blacks, don't complain*
> *You're better than them, you been born with white skin,"*
>   *they explain*

"Only a Pawn in Their Game"
Bob Dylan, 1963

Until 1967, marriages between Blacks and Whites were prohibited in Alabama. The US Supreme Court had to force the state to abolish that law.

> *What are you doing, Alabama?*
> *You got the rest of the Union*
> *To help you along*
> *What's going wrong?*

"Alabama"
Neil Young, 1971

This comment made by Neil Young on his 1972 album,

Harvest, was not well received. Two years later, Lynyrd Skynyrd's white trash state anthem "Sweet Home Alabama", responded:

> *I heard Mr. Young sing about her*
> *I heard ole Neil put her down*

"Sweet Home Alabama"
Lynyrd Skynyrd, 1974

In the context of the Good Old Boys and the Ku Klux Klan, lines like "I hope Neil Young will remember / A Southern man don't need him around anyhow..." are nothing short of a threat of murder. Young had previously recorded the following as well:

> *Southern man, better keep your head!*
> *Don't forget what your Good Book said!*
> *Southern change gonna come at last*
> *Now your crosses are burning fast...*
>
> *I saw cotton and I saw black*
> *Tall white mansions and little shacks*
> *Southern man, when will you pay them back?*
>
> *Lilly Belle, your hair is golden brown*
> *I've seen your black man comin' 'round*
> *How long? How long?*

"Southern Man"
Neil Young, 1970

Naturally, many Southern men were of the opinion that some progressive-minded Canadian immigrant like Young should mind his own business. But despite all this—and this must surely say something interesting about pop stars of that era and the rock and roll culture surrounding them—Neil Young and the members of Lynyrd Skynyrd remained lifelong friends. The latter enjoyed strutting around in Neil Young T-shirts and Young often playing "Sweet Home Alabama" on stage.

In "Southern Man" Neil Young really hit every nerve: referring to cross burnings, the white robes of the KKK, moral and financial debts, reparations, and even to an illicit relationship between a White woman and a Black man, probably the greatest possible provocation for a redneck. Hence the threat from Lynyrd Skynyrd whose song continues like this:

> *Now Muscle Shoals has got The Swampers*
> *And they've been known to pick a song*
>   *or two*
> *They pick me up when I'm feeling blue*

The Swampers were a loose formation of exceptional, White studio musicians, also named the Muscle Shoals Rhythm Section, from Muscle Shoals, Alabama. Their recording studio was in neighboring Sheffield along the Tennessee River. They can be heard on more than 500 records released since 1967. But even more important than the reference to the Muscle Shoals Rhythm Section is the reference to Governor George Wallace in the final verse:

> *Sweet home Alabama (oh, sweet home)*
> *Where the skies are so blue*
> *And the governor's true*
> *Sweet home Alabama (lordy)*

> *Lord I'm comin' home to you, yeah, yeah,*
> *Montgomery's got the answer*

In November 1962, this proud racist was elected governor for the first time, capturing ninety-six percent of ballots cast. In his inauguration speech in January, 1963, he infamously declared, "I say segregation now, segregation tomorrow, segregation forever." In the same year President Kennedy sent the National Guard to Tuscaloosa, Alabama, to have Wallace removed from the door of the university where he tried to keep two Black students from registering.

The song's fourth verse starts: "In Birmingham they love the governor." But if you listen closely, the backing vocals are: "Boo, hoo, hoo!" And, as quoted above, at the very end of the song we hear: "Montgomery's got the answer."

This line, tossed into the fade out, can only refer to the civil rights march led by Martin Luther King from Selma to Montgomery to protest segregation. The Freedom Marchers, who made three attempts to do this in 1965, were brutally clubbed down by police on "Bloody Sunday", March 7, 1965, and stopped by force twice. But the third time, when 3,200 protestors left Selma, their ranks grew to more than 25,000 marchers along the way. This time, on March 25, they did reach the capital, Montgomery. Today, these marches are considered the turning point of the civil rights movement in the US. Since the late fifties there had been confrontations over the registration of Black voters in Selma. In 1963 and 1964, the struggle escalated. The local authorities ("to serve and protect") reacted with arrests, torture, and shootings.

While all this was happening, much of White America was

preoccupied with the Gemini space program, designed to lay the groundworks for putting a man on the Moon. In 1961, President Kennedy had promised to land "a man on the moon and return him safely to Earth" before the 1960s were over. So, when Gemini 4 first launched two astronauts, James McDivitt and Ed White, for four days in orbit, it fired the imagination of America's White middle class much more than the civil rights struggle of its Black fellow citizens.

> *Think of all the hate there is in Red China!*
> *Then take a look around to Selma, Alabama!*
> *Ah, you may leave here for four days in space*
> *But when you return, it's the same old place*

"Eve of Destruction"
P.F. Sloan, 1965

This sardonic *bon mot* about "four days in space" was echoed by Gil Scott-Heron on the occasion of the first moon landing. His comment: "A rat done bit my sister Nell with whitey on the moon."

The highly esteemed father of the American Songbook, Stephen Foster, wrote a famous song in 1848. It is both the oldest and most popular song about Alabama:

> *I come from Alabama with my banjo on my knee*
> *I'm goin' to Louisiana, my true love for to see*
> *It rained all night the day I left, the weather it was dry*
> *The sun so hot I froze to death. Susanna, don't you cry!*
>
> *Oh! Susanna, do not cry for me!*

I come from Alabama with my banjo on my knee

I jumped aboard the telegraph
  and traveled down the river
Electric fluid magnified,
  and killed five hundred niggers
The bullgine bust, the horse ran off,
  I really thought I'd die
I shut my eyes to hold my breath.
Susanna, don't you cry!

I had a dream the other night,
when everything was still
I thought I saw Susanna dear,
a-comin' down the hill
The buckwheat cake was in her mouth,
a tear was in her eye
I says, "I've come in from the South.
Susanna, don't you cry!"

"Oh! Susanna"
Stephen Foster, 1848

What is striking here is not so much the nonsense of the first two stanzas, but the nonchalance with which five hundred "niggers" are killed. "Bullgine" is railroad slang for "steam engine".

The suffering of African Americans is a longstanding curse in the history of Alabama, as illustrated in this early example of White racism. It took another hundred years to culminate in the March on Montgomery. In 1933, the great ballad hunter and music ethnologist Alan Lomax recorded a song called "Black Betty" in a Texas prison. The words, which were recorded on aluminum cylinders back then, are very difficult to understand. But I've done my best to transcribe them here:

> *Black Betty, bamalam!*
> *Oh, Black Betty, bamalam!*
>
> *Black Betty, where d'you come from? Bamalam!*
> *Black Betty, where d'you come from? Bamalam!*
> *Well I come from Tuscaloosa, bamalam!*
> *Well, I'm going to Texarcana, bamalam!*
>
> *Black Betty, what's your number? Bamalam!*
> *Black Betty, what's your number? Bamalam!*
> *Seven hundred and fifty, bamalam!*
> *Seven hundred and fifty, bamalam!*
>
> *Oh Lord, Black Betty, bamalam!*
> *Oh Lordy, Black Betty, bamalam!*
>
> *Black Betty had a baby, bamalam!*
> *Black Betty had a baby, bamalam!*
> *And the damn thing crazy, bamalam!*
> *And the damn thing crazy, bamalam!*
>
> *Ah, she dipped its head in gravy, bamalam!*
> *Ah, she dipped its head in gravy, bamalam!*
> *Oh Lord, Black Betty, bamalam!*
> *Oh Lordy, Black Betty, bamalam!*
>
> *Black Betty, where she come from? Bamalam!*
> *Black Betty, where she come from? Bamalam!*
> *Black Betty, where she come from? Bamalam!*
> *Black Betty, where she come from? Bamalam!*
>
> *Oh Lordy, Black Betty, bamalam!*

Oh Lordy, Black Betty, bamalam!

Now, the baby had blue eyes, bamalam!
Oh, the baby had blue eyes, bamalam!
Well, it must have been the captain's, bamalam!
Well, it must have been the captain's, bamalam!

Oh Lordy, Black Betty, bamalam!
Oh Lordy, Black Betty, bamalam!

"Black Betty"
traditional, probably 19th century

Even as early as the 1930s, there were countless versions of this song. Leadbelly, too, had recorded it. Its origin and contents are the subject of speculation. It probably is derived from an English marching song from the 18th century. Black Betty most likely was a cannon or musket before she turned into a pregnant detainee. Either one would have been embraced by a soldier in war. This theory is supported by the onomatopoetic "bamalam" which seems to refer to the sounds of battle. In Washington, D.C., Black slang, "bama" means "backwards," often meaning "country." But of course, "bamalam" also triggers the connotation of "Alabam." However, "black betties" were also the whips used to dehumanize prisoners in the penitentiaries of the South.

Be that as it may, what interests us here is the bringing together of power, race, and sexuality. The song sketches all of it very clearly with just a few words. And, of course, to most people this song is not known as a cryptic field recording from the 1930s, but rather as the biggest hit of the white Southern hard rock band Ram Jam in 1977. Ram Jam preserves the character of the text, yet allows some changes. The story of prisoners, racism, and abuse now morph into a kind of love story about a very erotic Black Betty from Birmingham, Alabama:

> *She's from Birmingham, bamalam!*
> *Way down in Alabam', bamalam!*
>
> *Well, she's shakin' that thing, bamalam!*
> *Boy, she makes me sing, bamalam!*
> *Whoa, Black Betty, bamalam!*

"Black Betty"
Traditional/Ram Jam, 1977

Even the English band Humble Pie pulled from the fate of Black inmates in Alabama. "Alabama 69", however, is not about the state of Alabama in the year 1869 or 1969, but about Alabama State Route 69 built in 1940 and constructed by work gangs of Black prisoners sentenced to forced labor, as was still customary at the time in the US.

> *I come from Alabama,*
> *and I work a ten-pound hammer*
> *And my woman's picking cotton*
> *for the boss man on the hill*
> *They work us till they break our back*
> *Beat us 'cause our skin is black*
> *I guess I'll have to slave till*
> *they whip us in the grave*

"Alabama '69"
Humble Pie, 1969

Folklore from Alabama is mostly about suppression, random violence, penitentiaries, and forced labor:

> *Down in the valley, valley so low*
> *Late in the evening hear the wind blow!*
> *Hear the wind blow, love, hear the wind blow!*
> *Late in the evening, hear the wind blow!*
>
> *Write me a letter, send it by mail!*
> *Send it in care of Birmingham Jail*
> *Birmingham Jail, dear, Birmingham Jail*
> *Send it in care of Birmingham Jail!*
>
> *Roses love sunshine, violets love dew*
> *Angels in heaven know I love you*
> *Know I love you, dear, know I love you*
> *Angels in heaven know I love you*

"Down in the Valley"
Traditional, around 1925

Martin Luther King Jr. also sat in a Birmingham jail due to his participation in demonstrations against segregation. It was from there that he wrote an open letter to his congregation under the title "The Negro Is Your Brother" on April 16, 1963. "I am in Birmingham because injustice is here." These words became famous and neatly summarized the situation in Alabama. Five months later, on the 15th of September 1962, the Ku Klux Klan bombed a Black Baptist church in Birmingham, murdering four Black girls and injuring twenty others. The Black librarian and poet Dudley Randall published the following poem in response. It was set to music by folk singer Jerry Moore as "The Ballad of Birmingham", which became one of the most important anthems of the civil rights movement. In the song, a little girl asks her mother whether she may go and "march the streets of Birmingham in a Freedom March today?" The mother tells her that that is too dangerous but she would be allowed to go to church instead. The little girl dresses up for church:

> *She has combed and brushed her night-dark hair*
> *And bathed rose petal sweet*
> *And drawn white gloves on her small brown hands*
> *And white shoes on her feet*

The mother, happy "to know her child was in the sacred place" suddenly hears an explosion. She runs through the streets of Birmingham, frantically calling her daughter.

> *She clawed through bits of glass and brick*
> *Then lifted out a shoe.*
> *"Oh, here's the shoe my baby wore*
> *But, baby, where are you?"*

"The Ballad of Birmingham"
Dudley Randall and Jerry Moore, 1967

Alabama is always portrayed in the blues as hell on earth, as an abyss of violence and abuse:

> *I never will go back to Alabama,*
> *'cause that is not the place for me*
> *You know, they killed my sister and my brother,*
> *and the whole world let them peoples go down there free*
>
> *Alabama, Alabama, why do you wanna be so mean?*
> *You got my people behind a barbwire fence.*

I never will love Alabama,
Alabama seem to never have loved poor me

"Alabama Blues"
J.B. Lenoir, 1965

But Birmingham, Alabama, was once the most important railroad hub of the Deep South after Atlanta. The most popular mythical train of all American folklore, the Wabash Cannonball (often identified with the Rock Island Line) used to call it home:

Well, listen to the rumble,
the rattle and the roar!
Hear the mighty rush of the engine,
hear the lonesome hobo call!
Ridin' the rods and brakebeams
on the Wabash Cannonball.

She rolled into Birmingham
on a cold December day

Here's to Daddy Claxton,
may his name forever stand!
Always be remembered
in the courts of Alabam'
When his earthly days are over
and the curtains round him fall
They carry him home to glory
on the Wabash Cannonball

"The Wabash Cannonball"
Traditional/Townes Van Zandt,
late 19th Century/1993

It is not really clear who Daddy Claxton was. Some say he was a famous late 19th century attorney in Alabama who advocated for the rights of the poor and downtrodden. Others say the name refers to the country singer Roy Acuff, whose middle name was Claxton. Acuff had made the song famous. Anyway, you drive through Alabama as fast as you can if there is no reason for you to stop. This is how the Rolling Stones did it:

> *Wham, bam, Birmingham!*
> *Alabam' don't give a damn*

> "Rip This Joint"
> Jagger/Richards, 1972

Get in and get out quickly. That's also how Chuck Berry did it on the way to the promised land of California (repurposing the melody of The Wabash Cannonball):

> *We had a motor trouble that turned into a struggle*
> *Halfway across Alabam'*
> *And that 'hound broke down and left us all stranded*
> *In downtown Birmingham*
> *Straight away, I bought me a through train ticket*
>
> *And I was on that midnight flier out of Birmingham*
> *Smoking into New Orleans*

> "Promised Land"
> Chuck Berry, 1964

The message here is clear: Get out of Birmingham as fast as you can. Don't get stranded here. Berry and the Stones knew what they were talking about. Elvis, however, could still find his destiny in Mobile, Alabama. But Elvis was neither Black nor a dirty British junkie.

> *So, I slept in the hobo jungles*
> *Roamed a thousand miles of track*
> *Till I found myself in Mobile, Alabama*
> *At a club they call "Big Jack's"*
> *A little four-piece band was jammin'*
> *So, I took my guitar and I sat in*

"Guitar Man"
Jerry Reed, 1967

Mobile is the most important port city of Alabama. It is also, just as a little aside, the only American city that found grace in the eyes of Henry Miller. The name has nothing to do with mobility. Rather it is derived from a Choctaw word for the name of the tribe that once lived there. Just like Birmingham and Montgomery, Mobile has been plagued over many generations by racial segregation, discrimination, violence, pogroms, and civil rights struggles. The city is also home to the oldest Mardi Gras carnival in the US. Mobile was founded in 1703 by the French as the capital of Louisiana. A hundred years before, Napoleon had sold the huge territory to the US for very little money. There had been a Mardi Gras in Mobile, Alabama, fifteen years before New Orleans was even founded.

Alabama's reputation—even abroad—is reflected in "Alabama Song" written in 1927 by Bertolt Brecht and set to music by Kurt Weill in the same year for their opera *The Rise and Fall of the City of Mahagonny*. To my knowledge, it is the only poem ever written in English by Brecht:

> *Well, show me the way*
> *To the next whiskey bar!*
> *Oh, don't ask why!*
> *For if we don't find*
> *The next whiskey bar*
> *I tell you, we must die*
>
> *Oh, moon of Alabama!*
> *We now must say good-bye*
> *We've lost our good old mama*
> *And must have whiskey, oh, you know why*

"Alabama Song"
Bertolt Brecht and Kurt Weill, 1927

Some fans of The Doors probably thought this was an original song by Jim Morrison and The Doors about whiskey and sex on Sunset Boulevard. So naturally did it come across. But it was just another example of how songs continue to live and migrate from one generation to another, one culture to another.

Economically, Alabama is part of the Cotton Belt. Culturally, it belongs to the Bible Belt. Sex was never discussed in public. But drugs and their generous consumption played a role in Alabama and have always been a public talking point there:

> *Alabama high test*
> *Got me in a big mess*
> *Higher than a wild cat*
> *Runnin' from the wolf pack*
> *They're gonna put me in the slammer*
> *If they catch me with that Alabama high test*

> *65 Southbound, cruisin with a half-pound*
> *Blue lights spinnin' 'round, better put the hammer down*
>
> *Drug bust, disgust, plead with the circuit judge*
> *"Son, don't be coy, send you up the river, boy"*
> *Jump suit, chain gang, shackles on my feet and hand*
> *Standin' on I-65 wishin' I was rolling by with*
> *Alabama high test*

"Alabama High Test"
Old Crow Medicine Show, 2008

These stories about drug use, as funny as they may be here, are not altogether fictional. Alabama is the state with the highest number of car accidents under the influence of alcohol. The opioid crisis is raging in Birmingham. Yet great artists hail from there, such as Sun Ra, Odetta, and Emmylou Harris. And although the steel industry is nearly dead, people still live their lives there. Nobody described them better than Randy Newman. In "Birmingham", he slips into the character of an early 1970s roller in a steel mill there, proud to "earn my living with my hands" and provide for his wife and family:

> *We live in a three-room house*
> *With a pepper tree*
> *I work all day in the factory*
> *That's alright with me*
>
> *You can travel 'cross this entire land*
> *But there ain't no place like Birmingham*

"Birmingham"
Randy Newman, 1974

BALTIMORE

*It's raining in Baltimore, Baby
But everything else is the same*

"Raining in Baltimore"
Counting Crows, 1993

The next logical place to go from Alabama, geographically and culturally, would be its neighboring state, Mississippi. But before we go there, I want to insert a little chapter on Baltimore. That's because Birmingham and Baltimore have striking similarities despite being so far apart on the map.

On the one hand, Baltimore reigns as one of the oldest and most venerable cities in the country. Although it was only founded in 1729, Baltimore is seen in the same league as Annapolis, Boston, and Philadelphia as one of the first commercial cities in the colonies. Its old mercantile families are as close to royalty as you can get in the US. Baltimore once was an important business center with a bourgeois upper class and the self-confidence and sophistication one would associate with that. However, all its splendor and bourgeois grandeur has faded away. Today's Baltimore is nothing but a shadow of its former self. It lives off its former glory. Now the specific charm Baltimore exudes is more due to a rather picturesque decay than actual importance.

On the other hand, Baltimore excels in one of the highest murder rates in the nation. A city of half a million, it endured 337 homicides in 2021. That is eleven times that of New York City (or sixty-five times higher than in Germany or other European countries) per capita. But we will come back to that later.

It has been said before that the American petite bourgeoisie suffered from a complex of egalitarianism caused by the pretenses the society was built upon, and that they had a peculiar weakness for European nobility and a tendency to turn pop singers and baseball players into pseudo-royalty. As exaggerated as this theory may sound, Baltimore is its best proof. People from Baltimore were once considered prestigious, respected, and wealthy:

> *The lady came from Baltimore*
> *All she wore was lace*
> *She didn't know that I was poor*
>
> *I was sent to steal her money*
> *Take her rings and run*

"The Lady Came from Baltimore"
Tim Hardin, 1967

Baltimore once was home to old money, nepotism, and pride, stylish, arrogant, and racist to the bone. In his song "The Lonesome Death of Hattie Carroll" of 1963, Bob Dylan delivers a detailed and matter-of-fact description of what had actually happened in the early morning of February 9 of the same year at a ball at the Emerson Hotel in Baltimore. The drunken 24-year-old William Zantzinger (as his real name was spelled), son of rich parents and himself already the owner of a 600-acre tobacco farm attacked several Black hotel employees and his own wife with a cane. On the spur of the moment, because he just felt like it, he beat to death Hattie Carroll, a 51-year-old mother of nine. Zantzinger was taken into custody for first degree murder. But as he had "high office relations in the politics of Maryland", he was released on bail and served a mere six months in prison for the murder. Had he been African American, he would most certainly have been given the death penalty. Capital punishment was not abolished in Maryland until 2013. Until his peaceful passing in 2009, Zantzinger lived a quiet and undisturbed life as a convinced and passionate racist.

Baltimore's special reputation is not only based on its more or less sophisticated old money. Moreover, there is a traditional historic and patriotic importance associated with the city.

Two significant anthems were written here, and both are more or less bizarre. In 1861, Maryland's blood-thirsty state anthem (until 2021) "Maryland, My Maryland", and in 1814, the national anthem (since 1931) "The Star-Spangled Banner", which is no less aggressive. During the Battle of Baltimore in the midst of the War of 1812, Francis Scott Key had written a poem mocking the English. There was no need for a new musical composition, it was conveniently provided by the enemy. The patriotic diatribe was simply sung to the tune of the well-known English drinking song "To Anacreon in Heaven" by John Stafford Smith. That's how the anthem of the United States came to be. Today only the first of four verses of the beautiful old British song remain due to the blood-thirsty and militaristic character and anti-British sentiment of the original.

> *Oh, say can you see*
> *By the dawn's early light*
> *What so proudly we hailed*
> *At the twilight's last gleaming?*
>
> *Whose broad stripes and bright stars*
> *Through the perilous fight*
> *O'er the ramparts we watched*
> *Were so gallantly streaming?*
>
> *No refuge could save the hireling and slave*
> *From the terror of flight or the gloom of the grave*
>
> *And the rocket's red glare*
> *The bombs bursting in air*
> *Gave proof through the night*
> *That our flag was still there*
> *Oh, say, does that star-spangled*
> *Banner yet wave*
> *O'er the land of the free*
> *And the home of the brave?*

"The Star-Spangled Banner"
John Stafford Smith and Francis Scott Key, 1727/1814

The lyricist, Scott Francis Key, had run away from the attacking British soldiers in the Battle of Bladensburg—also given the moniker "Bladensburg Race"—in 1814. The line about the "hireling and slave" was his outraged reaction to the British actually giving freedom to every runaway slave that fought with them.

The story of how the former state anthem of Maryland came to be is even stranger. It was sung to the tune of the beloved German Christmas carol "O Tannenbaum". The carol was first turned into a battle song of hatred by the Confederates in their struggle to preserve slavery. It then became the official state anthem of Maryland in 1939. The contrast between the peaceful Christmas tune and the bellicose lyrics creates a strange tension.

> *The despot's heel is on thy shore, Maryland!*
> *His torch is at thy temple door, Maryland!*
> *Avenge the patriotic gore that flecked the streets*
>   *of Baltimore*
> *And be the battle queen of yore, Maryland!*
> *My Maryland!*
>
> *Thou wilt not cower in the dust, Maryland!*
> *Thy beaming sword shall never rust, Maryland!*
> *Remember Carroll's sacred trust,*
>   *remember Howard's warlike thrust*
> *And all thy slumberers with the just, Maryland!*
> *My Maryland!*
>
> *I see the blush upon thy cheek, Maryland!*
> *For thou wast ever bravely meek, Maryland!*
> *But lo! There surges forth a shriek*
>   *from hill to hill, from creek to creek*
> *Potomac calls to Chesapeake, Maryland!*
> *My Maryland!*
>
> *Thou wilt not yield the vandal toll, Maryland!*
> *Thou wilt not crook to his control, Maryland!*
> *Better the fire upon thee roll, better the blade,*
>   *the shot, the bowl*
> *Than crucifixion of the soul, Maryland!*

My Maryland!
I hear the distant thunder hum, Maryland!
The Old Line's bugle, fife, and drum, Maryland!
She is not dead, nor deaf, nor dumb. Huzza!
She spurns the Northern scum!
She breathes! She burns! She'll come! She'll come!
Maryland! My Maryland!

"Maryland, My Maryland"
Silesian Folk Song, 16th Century /
James Ryder Randall, 1861

The despot in this context is the North who wanted to deprive proud Maryland of its freedom, of its freedom to hold slaves. Shortly before the beginning of the Civil War some US soldiers in Baltimore were attacked by forces loyal to the South. The skirmish resulted in some casualties on the side of the federal forces. This is the event alluded to in the line about the "patriotic gore that flecked the streets of Baltimore."

Of course, even the most radical patriots in Maryland today feel a little embarrassed by these gory words, the reference to President Lincoln as the "scum of the North" and the use of a world-famous Christmas melody. Using that melody was not very imaginative, especially because the exact same tune is also used for the state anthems of Florida, Iowa, and Michigan. All attempts to replace the anthem with something more palatable had failed until 2021, when the state legislature finally voted to abolish the spiteful tune. It had taken more than ten tries over four decades.

Baltimore, as was mentioned before, has very little reason to be self-confident unless you take pride in living in the most dangerous city in the country. What has become of the once proud jewel in the heart of the Eastern Seaboard, so full of impressive monumental architecture, elements of which have survived until today? How could it go to the dogs so quickly?

From its founding until the 1960s, the city and many of its inhabitants had it good. Baltimore was an important shipping port and an industrial hub. The steel industry attracted workers and their families from all over the country. Baltimore quickly grew to more than a million residents. It promised a high standard of living and a certain flair.

In "The Streets of Baltimore", Bobby Bare tells the striking but not uncommon story of a Tennessee farmer whose wife longs for the city life. He sells the farm "to take my woman where she longed to be" and buys one way train tickets to Baltimore. And indeed, she is enthralled.

> *Her heart was filled with laughter*
> *when she saw those city lights*
> *She said the prettiest place on earth*
> *is Baltimore at night*

He finds a job in a factory and even buys a modest house in the city.

> *Yet every night when I came home*
> *with every muscle sore*
> *She would drag me through the streets*
> *of Baltimore*

> *I soon learned she loved those bright lights*
> *much more than she loved me*

In the end, he returns to Tennessee...

> *On that same train*
> *that brought me here before*

While my baby walks the streets of Baltimore

"The Streets of Baltimore"
Bobby Bare, 1966

In the 1960s and '70s the steel industry found it increasingly difficult to keep up with the competition from Southeast Asia. Disappointment began to set in. Working conditions declined and environmental pollution became unbearable.

My wife had an uncle that worked ever' day
In a nut and bolt factory up in Baltimore

I got me a job a-carrying hod
Breathing the smog of old Baltimore

That dirt, it was black and the work hurt my back

The smell of the bay, the buildings of gray
Was more than I bargained for

"No Milk and Honey in Baltimore"
Buck Owens, 1970

The American steel industry's last victim of this globalization was the Bethlehem Steel Corporation, which had once been the second largest producer of steel in the country. As early as 1971, it laid off three thousand Sparrows Point steel mill workers in Baltimore. Then the company installed a new blast furnace and things seemed to improve. However, in 2001 Bethlehem Steel gave up the fight and filed for bankruptcy. But the struggle was just beginning for Bethlehem Steel's former employees and their families, their fight for survival, a fight they could only lose. Rollers don't evolve into coders very easily, nor into robotics engineers. There were no offers for professional re-training to speak of. In fact, there were not many alternatives to speak of at all except selling drugs. To this day, ninety percent of the few legitimate jobs Baltimore has to offer are in the low-paid service industries.

The low-income parts of town that housed the majority of mainly African American steel workers were now turning into slums, where half the residents do not even have a high school degree. It hit the younger generation hardest, as it often does. One of the few ways to make money in neighborhoods like Sandtown was, of course, to deal drugs. And demand was up. Baltimore was abandoned and left to fend for itself.

> *Hard times in the city*
> *In a hard town by the sea*
> *There ain't nothin' here for free*
>
> *The city's dyin'*
> *And they don't know why*
>
> *Oh, Baltimore!*
> *Man, it's hard just to live*

"Baltimore"
Randy Newman, 1977

Things only got worse because anyone who could leave did.

> *If I had my way, I'd go home today*
> *For there's no milk and honey here in Baltimore*

"No Milk and Honey in Baltimore"
Buck Owens, 1970

Only those who had no hope were left behind. The American television series *The Wire* (2002-2008), for instance, provides some useful insight into life (and death) in the projects and ghettos of Baltimore.

The eighteenth-century Scottish economist, Adam Smith, famously suggested there is an invisible hand of market forces that brings out the best in a society, that the additive result of many competing egotisms leads to the best of all possible worlds. But a thoughtful look at Baltimore makes clear the consequences of this irresponsible notion.

To be fair, though, "the invisible hand" is not the core of Smith's thought. But it has become the battle cry of neo-liberalists, people Smith himself would probably have been appalled by. Nevertheless, Baltimore is an illustration of the consequences of unchecked competing egoisms in a racist and violent society.

> *What this town was entirely built upon…*
> *It's a bullet hole that'll steal your soul*
> *And roll you for your money and your diamonds*
>
> "Baltimore Blues No. 1"
> Deer Tick, 2007

Street riots broke out in 2015 after the Baltimore police broke the neck of a Black man who was already in custody. Ever since, silent desperation and hopelessness, drug addiction and criminal gangs, have controlled the streets of Baltimore. Anger turned into despondence. People have tried many things since to get the city's problems under control. One can pretend they don't exist or accept the unravelling. Or you do both at the same time and try to see the positive in the misery. "Good Morning, Baltimore", the opening number of the over-the-top musical, *Hairspray*, tries to do just that.

The plot of *Hairspray* is set in 1962 and based on Baltimore native John Waters' movie of the same name. The film came before the musical. Tracy Turnblad is the main character. (Did the author know German and intentionally choose this name which translates as "turn the page"?) The chubby girl is eternally optimistic and always believes things will go her way soon. But the main character is really the city of Baltimore itself as seen through Tracy's eyes.

"Good Morning, Baltimore" describes Tracy's route to school, but also Tracy herself and her dream of becoming a dancer. The song strikes a fine balance between the joy of living in the moment and ironic resignation.

> *The rats on the street*
> *All dance around my feet*
> *So, don't hold me back!*
> *'Cause today all my dreams will come true*
> *There's the flasher who lives next door*
> *There's the bum on his barroom stool*
> *They wish me luck on my way to school*
> *I know every step, I know every song*
> *Someday, when I take to the floor*
> *The world's gonna wake up and see,*
> *Baltimore and me...*

"Good Morning, Baltimore"
Marc Shaiman and Scott Michael Wittman, 2002

Here the fates of two mightily challenged entities (Tracy and Baltimore) are seamlessly knit together. No more will the city of Baltimore turn a new leaf than the heavy-set girl will become a ballerina. But in spite of their bleak prospects, the situation is not hopeless. Not yet, anyway. When Tracy sings

"I know every step" she is not just referring to her well-studied dance routines. She also knows the streets, people, sights and sounds of the city. That is the blessing and the curse of living in a small town, even of the small town that Baltimore has become against its will after its economic collapse and the shrinking of its population that followed.

> *And when I walk down the street*
> *All the faces that I meet I've met before*
> *Welcome to Smalltimore!*

"Welcome to Smalltimore"
Howard Markman, 2010

The city's boredom and uniformity has also been perfectly captured by one of Baltimore's greatest sons, Frank Zappa (who could share the title with Bill Frisell, Barry Levinson, Upton Sinclair and John Waters). He asks the probing question in "What's New in Baltimore?"

> *Hey! What's new in Baltimore?*
> *I don't know…*
> *Better go back and find out!*

"What's New in Baltimore"
Frank Zappa, 1981

Just before he died in 1993, he was given an answer by Adam Duritz, front man of the Counting Crows, also born in Baltimore. The answer was: "nothing."

> *It's raining in Baltimore, fifty miles East*
> *Where you should be, no one's around*

> *It's raining in Baltimore, baby*
> *But everything else is the same*

"Raining in Baltimore"
Counting Crows, 1993

Nothing had changed in Baltimore. Stagnation and depression dominate the town. The beauty of Baltimore has long only been mentioned ironically.

> *Keep Baltimore beautiful!*
>   *It wouldn't look so pretty if I cried...*
> *The city looks like someone took*
>   *the sunshine out of town...*

"Keep Baltimore Beautiful"
Skeeter Davis, 1969

Be that as it may, if something is really regarded as out of fashion and homely, you can be sure that sooner or later Madison Avenue or some fashion designer will pick up on it in their desperate hunt for an unheard-of new trend. Sometimes all it takes is a few self-important hipsters to proclaim yesterday's outdated and embarrassing fashion as tomorrow's new hotness. And this is what is happening to Baltimore now. Its pleasantly nondescript blandness has recently been glossed over with a little bit of hope for a new beginning. Craft beer breweries with their unpalatable IPAs, nice beer gardens and cellars, hipster cafes and more have begun to finally change the character of the city. No wonder, because Baltimore is only 40 minutes from prospering, but expensive, Washington DC. It is also conveniently located on the route to New York City. And that is enough to proclaim it the "new Brooklyn," the world's hipster capital.

Is there any irony in this? The line that Baltimore is really not that far from where one wants to be, makes us think so. Also, that Baltimore was at least better than New Jersey.

> *Baltimore is the new Brooklyn*
> *It's just a short train ride away*
> *from where you really want to be*
> *But no one really wants to be down*
> *in Washington DC...*
> *Well, it's much better than New Jersey*

> "Baltimore Is the New Brooklyn"
> JC Brooks & The Uptown Sound, 2009

But that is an old saw. Brooklyn has long been a part of Baltimore. Founded in 1853, this other Brooklyn is the southernmost neighborhood of Baltimore, right at the mouth of the Patapsco River, close to the Baltimore-Washington International Thurgood Marshall Airport, used by more Washingtonians than Baltimoreans. And that will not change any time soon. Washington keeps booming and gentrifying its last slums, whereas Baltimore keeps shrinking slowly despite its craft beer and new hipster hype cycle.

MISSISSIPPI

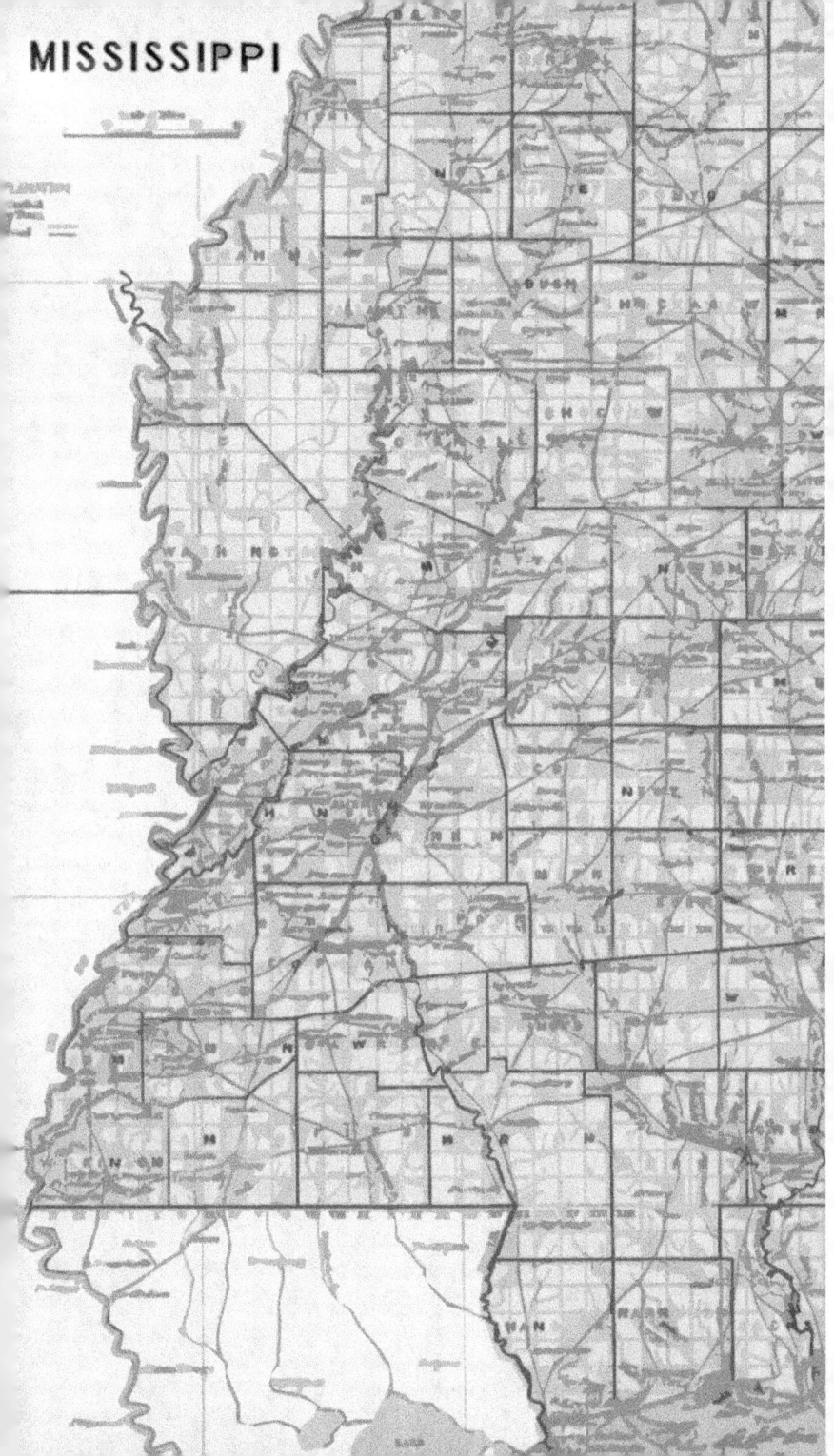

MISSISSIPPI

Only thing I did wrong
Was stayed in Mississippi a day too long

> From an old blues song
> recorded by Alan Lomax in
> the Mississippi Parchman
> Farm prison in 1947 or 1948,
> quoted by Bob Dylan in his
> song "Mississippi", 2000

We continue our journey where we left off before taking a small detour to the East Coast: in the Deep South, in Mississippi, heartland of the blues.

When children play hide-and-go-seek, or want to know how long it takes for a rock to hit the bottom of a well, they count, "One Mississippi, two Mississippi..." For most

Americans who are not from Mississippi or a neighboring state, this is the first and most formative association with the state named after the greatest river in the nation. The Missouri is longer but carries less water. The next immediate thought people have is equally persistent, but less playful. They think of the state of Mississippi as a failed state, the poor house of the nation. A place that cannot be helped. A land full of poverty, bigotry, lack of education, racism, and backwardness.

At the same time, Mississippi, in particular the Mississippi Delta, rightfully claims to be the cradle of the blues. And the blues, in its pure form or as the precursor of jazz, pop and rock music, may well be considered the greatest cultural achievement of North America since the beginning of its colonization.

The Delta is not the mouth of the Mississippi, but rather it is the leaf-shaped backcountry between the Yazoo River in the East and the Mississippi in the West, south of Memphis, and north of Vicksburg. This region is considered the birthplace of the blues. In the late 19th and early 20th centuries, this is where field hollers with a call and response structure developed from West African pentatonic tradition. A song leader chants, and the choir repeats the line. Under the influence of European folk songs and church hymns, this was slowly forged into the classic twelve-bar form of the blues. It shares some similarity with the structure of Hegel's dialectic: a thesis is brought forward in four bars on the one chord. Then it is usually repeated verbatim, thus turning the first line into an implicit question in four bars on the fourth chord. That is followed by the apotheosis or synthesis with an answer in a four-bar cadence via the fifth chord back to the first chord, sometimes with the fourth chord in between and sometimes not. Before the pattern starts over again, there is usually a turnaround.

However, the Mississippi Delta not only produced the blues itself, it also shaped a unique style of blues. The peculiar, haunting mood of the Delta blues is partly the result of the tension between harmonic, melodic vocal phrases across wide intervals like in field hollers and rhythmical guitar accompaniment comprised of just a few notes, often of only one chord. Even after the commercialization of the blues, this is still clearly audible, for example in talking blues by John Lee Hooker or Lonnie Pitchford with his one-string guitar called a "diddley bow".

Mississippi spawned such an abundance of distinctly different blues greats that it can be regarded as an entire blues universe itself. It is the beginning and the end of rural blues. New Orleans, Kansas City, and New York may bring forward competing claims for their respective importance to the development of jazz. However, nobody would seriously question the singular role Mississippi had in shaping the blues. Texas may have developed its own unique guitar techniques. Chicago may have created electrified city blues and R&B. But that does not diminish the outstanding importance of Mississippi for the blues. Its backdrop is brutal slavery and segregation, the exploitation of Black laborers, the cruelty of Jim Crow laws, the lynching, the backwardness and isolation of the country, its feudal and paternalistic ways that have partly lingered on to this day. In the Delta, there is a peculiar Bible Belt mixture of bigotry and a devoted, charismatic Baptist faith. Its desolate, uniform landscape with nothing but a few clay hills and an endless, monotonous, flat hinterland, the brooding, humid heat—all of this results in an ambivalent, repulsive fascination with Mississippi. It is a miracle of breathtaking, unsettling beauty that music like the blues, indeed that an entire culture, could rise from this soil.

Americans don't like to call Mississippi a "failed state." They prefer to call it the "Lost South." Occasionally this also encompasses the neighboring states of Alabama and Louisiana. But the poorest of all states in the US is Mississippi. It went bankrupt as early as 1840, during the heyday of the agrarian economy based on slavery which so characterized Mississippi. Today, Mississippi has the lowest per capita income of any state. One fifth of the population lives below the poverty line, in some areas even fifty percent. Also, with regard to the average life expectancy, health care and education, Mississippi finishes last. Its crime rate has always been very high for a rural, agrarian region. Mississippi has always considered violence its preferred means of conflict resolution:

> *Well, I was born in Mississippi,*
> *and I don't take any stuff from you*
> *And if I hit you on your head, boy,*
> *it's got to make you black and blue*

"Mississippi Kid"
Lynyrd Skynyrd, 1973

European conquest, especially by the French, originally spread northward up the river. Today, the waterway continues to dominate life in the open landscape east and west of its lower section. "Mississippi" means "big river" in Chippewa. In literature and music, the Mississippi often serves as an image for life. The river calls for people to identify their own lives with its majestic and stubborn flow like in the global hit "Ol' Man River" by Jerome Kern and Oscar Hammerstein from 1927. Even in a well-meant song like this, the self-ascribed racist slur from today's point of view is hard to bear.

> *Niggers work on de Mississippi*
> *Niggers work while de White folks play*
> *Pullin' dose boats from de dawn to sunset*
>
> *Don't look up an' don't look down!*
> *You don' dare make de White boss frown*
> *Bend your knees an' bow your head!*
> *An' pull dat rope until you' dead!*
>
> *Let me go 'way from the Mississippi!*
> *Let me go 'way from de White man boss!*
>
> *Ol' man river, dat ol' man river*
> *He mus' know sumpin', but don't say nuthin'*
> *He jes' keeps rollin', he keeps on rollin' along*
>
> *He don' plant tater, he don' plant cotton*
> *An' dem dat plants 'em is soon forgotten*
> *But ol' man river, he jes' keeps rollin' along*
>
> *Ah gits weary an' sick of tryin'*
> *Ah'm tired of livin' an' skeered of dyin'*
> *But ol' man river, he jes' keeps rollin' along!*

"Ol' Man River"
Kern/Hammerstein, 1927

Here it is so clear that everything will always remain the same within the White, unjust, world of the South. The river, the "Old Man," will stoically continue to flow, long after all the *miserables* on its embankments have been worked to death and are long forgotten. The song was very popular for decades, although I suspect more so with Whites than with African Americans. The song was written by Whites and performed by either Black or White singers like Frank Sinatra for mostly White audiences. Although the lyrics were probably well intended, there is something paternalistic about them—like an aftertaste of Uncle Tom's Cabin.

People in the North got their first taste of more authentic music from Mississippi in the early 1950s when a legendary gospel group made it widely famous with White audiences. The Five Blind Boys of Mississippi even made it to the rhythm and blues charts with their big hit "Our Father".

When White people speak about the river it sounds very different from Black people. However, the one thing they have in common is that the big river is personified as a protagonist. Like the river, the song rambles on. The first-person narrator equates the river's upper and lower reaches with the ups and downs of his one-sided love affair with *that woman*, and

> *The tears that I cried for that woman are gonna flood you, big river.*

From the very beginning, everything is literally going south, downstream:

> *Well, I met her accidentally in St. Paul, Minnesota*
> *And it tore me up every time I heard her drawl,*
>   *southern drawl*
>
> *Then you took me to St. Louis later on down the river*

> *A freighter said she's been here, but she's gone, boy,*
> *she's gone*

> *Now, won't you batter down by Baton Rouge,*
> *River Queen, roll it on!*
> *Take that woman on down to New Orleans,*
> *New Orleans!*

In the end, both the big river and unrequited love have run their course. Together, they flow into the Gulf of Mexico.

> *Go on, I've had enough, dump my blues*
> *down in the gulf*
> *She loves you, big river, more than me*

"Big River"
Johnny Cash, 1957

The Mississippi is a life story, the All-American River. *She loves you, big river, more than me...* It ties the country together while dividing it at the same time into East and West. Historically, it has been the dividing line between the civilization of the older settlements and cities in the East and the ever-westward advancing and finally disappearing frontier. For centuries, the collective consciousness of the American nation has placed convention and tradition east of the river. On the other bank, in the West, lie adventure, the future and the Manifest Destiny most Americans continue to believe in to this day.

Many participated in building out the river's mythology. With his stories around Tom Sawyer and Huckleberry Finn, Mark Twain created bittersweet idyllic scenes of a footloose, free life on the banks of the river. The small-town setting of Twain's stories shows obvious parallels to Hannibal where the author spent his own childhood. John Fenimore Cooper's historical novels also contributed to the picture. And William Faulkner, winner of the Nobel Prize for literature, was from New Albany, Mississippi, and most of his writing is centered around the state, albeit not the river itself.

The Mississippi is the aorta of the South. The river also serves as the basis and source of life for the prairie states of the Midwest. However, the South is literally made of the fertile, alluvial land deposited by the river. In mythology, life often springs forth from river mud. Such is the case of the Indus Valley, the cradle of human civilization, just as for the sacred, primeval mud of the Nile that determined the fortune or failure of entire dynasties of pharaohs. Rabbi Löw kneaded the virgin mud of the Moldova River into the Golem. The blues, however, was baked of Mississippi mud. Mississippi Mud Steppers was the name of a hillbilly spin-off of the Mississippi Sheiks, who were very successful in the 1930s.

> *When the sun goes down, the tide goes out*
> *The people gather 'round and they all begin to shout*
> *"It's a treat to beat your feet on the Mississippi mud."*
>
> *What a dance do they do!*
> *They don't need no band*
> *They keep time by clappin' their hand*
> *When the people beat their feet on the Mississippi mud*

"Mississippi Mud"
Barry Harris for Bing Crosby, 1927

Mississippi is extremely rural. Churches, especially Baptist churches, play a major role in the countryside, not only in religious but also in social and cultural matters. The thin White upper crust of society is a member of the Episcopal Church. However, African Americans and the majority of White people are engaged in Baptist congregations. The Black churches tend to be rather emotional and ecstatic and filled with music, while White Baptists are more apt to be fundamentalist and reactionary.

There is only one major city in Mississippi, the largest city in the state, the capital, Jackson. And it is tiny with just 166,000 inhabitants. Overall, the state is very sparsely populated, with only three million inhabitants across 46,923 square miles, fifty percent less density than the US average. It is deepest backcountry in every respect. For most people in the countryside, a trip to Jackson resembles a grand tour. the duet "Jackson", immortalized by a live recording featuring Johnny and June Carter Cash just before they got married, is all about the tension between a boisterous husband and his skeptical wife. In the beginning of the song, they both believe a trip to Jackson could be beneficial to their marriage:

> *We got married in a fever,*
> *We've been talkin' 'bout Jackson,*
> *ever since the fire went out*

But then the husband gives it a different twist:

> *I'm goin' to Jackson,*
> *I'm gonna mess around*

As a response, his wife pours scorn on him:

> *Well, go on down to Jackson;*
> *go ahead and wreck your health!*
> *Go play your hand, you big-talkin' man,*
> *make a big fool of yourself!*

Unimpressed and unwavering, the husband answers the ridicule with delusions of grandeur:

> *When I breeze into that city,*
> *people gonna stoop and bow*
> *All them women gonna make me*
> *teach 'em what they don't know how*

How will the city, even a simple provincial town like Jackson, react to a boastful country bumpkin like this? His wife seems to know the answer:

> *They'll laugh at you in Jackson*

"Jackson"
Wheeler/Leiber, 1963

Again, we see a familiar pattern: the big, bad city as temptation and damnation. And, shockingly, they drink there too, just like in the rest of the South, and the women are looser than the Baptist preachers would like:

> *I'm sittin' in a bar tippling a jar in Jackson...*
> *There's many a barroom queen I've had in Jackson*
> *But I just can't seem to drink you off my mind*

"Country Honk"
Jagger/Richards, 1969

In the South, there is a lot of heavy drinking, but that's especially true in Mississippi, Alabama, Louisiana, and Arkansas. In the early days that meant moonshine with a high percentage of methyl. Folks also like to smoke marijuana, crystal meth, crack, and take fentanyl, uppers and downers, snort cocaine, sniff glue and shoot up with heroin. One of the most gifted drunks and most influential blues musicians of his time, along with Robert Johnson, was Charley Patton. He single-handedly forged the entire first generation of Delta blues musicians. Because of his restless life-style moving around in the Delta, playing joints and cheap hotels and flop houses, he informed the development and standardization of the blues as a musical and lyrical genre to an extent that cannot be overestimated. He was born one of twelve children in 1891 in the proximity of Bolton near Edwards, Mississippi. His family moved to Dockerey Plantation near Cleveland, Mississippi. Cleveland is right in the center of the Delta. Tommy Johnson and some other blues musicians also lived on Dockery Plantation, which had been built by workhands as an alternative to the rigid system of sharecropping in the Mississippi Delta.

When he began cutting records, Charley Patton moved near Clarksdale on Highway 61. There, he partnered with Son Sims, a rather uncouth backcountry fiddler. Clarksdale, in the southernmost part of the Delta, has the largest, most famous and most notorious prison in Mississippi. Perhaps calling it a "prison" is euphemistic. The old-fashioned term "penitentiary" is more accurate. It is a penal institution. The buildings are surrounded by cotton fields where the inmates serve their sentence of forced labor. They are also used for digging ditches or building roads. Almost all of them are African Americans. Basically, a large portion of the Black population of Mississippi went directly from slavery to the freedom of being exploited by the market economy, to political disenfranchisement by Jim Crow laws, as well as racist persecution by means of an imposing lynch law and the Ku Klux Klan. And it went on with the system of forced labor in the work camps. Of all the states in the Union, Mississippi has the highest percentage of African Americans, thirty-six percent. However, that does not mean that African Americans have ever held political power in Mississippi.

In 1865, when the 13th Amendment to the US Constitution prohibited slavery (but not penal labor, which is still legal in the United States), Mississippi voted against its ratification. It was finally ratified 130 years later, in 1995, and until 2013 slavery was legal under Mississippi law.

During the Civil War, Vicksburg, a small city at the southern end of the Delta, was besieged by Union troops from May to July of 1863. It was finally captured on July fourth. That marked the fall of the last important bastion of Confederate troops to surrender to Union soldiers. Even until long after World War II, many parts of Mississippi did not celebrate the day of American Independence. Even today, Vicksburg holds back on the holiday. There, it still tends to be seen as a day of the disgrace of defeat and humiliation and also the end of the system of slavery. Until 2020, Mississippi's flag incorporated the Confederate flag, making it the last state to boast the rebel symbol. That was more than folklore: it was a provocation against the Union and a plea for White Supremacy.

This notion of the superiority of the White race was long the official state ideology of Mississippi. There, Theodore Bilbo was, with a few interruptions, either senator or governor between 1916 and 1947. He was not only an outspoken anti-Semite, but also openly supported the legalization of lynching. For a long time, lynching had been considered a popular pastime among Whites in Mississippi. Animals were protected by offseason, but every day was hunting season for Black men:

> *Down in Mississippi where I come from [...]*
> *They had a huntin' season on a rabbit*
> *If you shoot him, you went to jail*
> *The season was always open on me*

> "Down In Mississippi"
> J.B. Lenoir, 1966

Even in the 1920s and 1930s, lynching was more popular in Mississippi than in any other state. Until the 1940s, the Ku Klux Klan ruled the state with impunity. In 1955, a 14-year-old Black boy named Emmett Till went to visit his uncle in Money, Mississippi. He was from Chicago, a city that was already much more emancipated.

> *'Twas down in Mississippi not so long ago*
> *When a young boy from Chicago town stepped*
>   *through a Southern door*

The song then details how Till was tortured to death by Whites in a most brutal way, supposedly for whistling at a White woman. The perpetrators were clearly identified, but an all-White jury found them innocent.

> *Two brothers, they confessed that they had killed*
>   *poor Emmett Till*
> *The jury found them innocent*

> *and the brothers they went free*
>
> *This song is just a reminder*
> *to remind your fellow man*
> *That this kind of thing still lives today*
> *in that ghost-robed Ku Klux Klan*

"Death of Emmett Till"
Bob Dylan, 1962

Till's mother insisted that the coffin be open at the funeral. The murder, but even more so photos of Till's battered and disfigured, swollen face, and—to some extent—Dylan's song, sparked national outrage that marked the beginning of the Civil Rights Movement.

The Mississippi Delta in its present form was created in the 19th and 20th centuries. The State built dams to transform into fertile farmland swamps that regularly flooded. The cheapest way to do so was to use prisoners sentenced to forced labor. Finally, the state built its own forced labor camp.

Parchman Farm, near Clarksdale in the Delta, is the largest Mississippi penitentiary. It is filled with mostly Black inmates who are forced to toil in unpaid hard labor as part of their punishment. The prison is about thirty miles southeast of Clarksdale on a large flat plain near the small town of Tutwiler.

A lone shack serves as the train station on the rail spur that leads to Parchman Farm. It is used to transport the prisoners to the largest camp in the Mississippi Department of Corrections. Here, the Yazoo River meets the Mississippi. Close by in Moorhead, the lines of the Southern Railroad cross those of the Yazoo Delta Railroad, the so-called Yellow Dog. This is where the great blues singer Bessie Smith met her grisly demise on September 26, 1937. On their way from Memphis to Clarksdale on Route 61, her boyfriend miscalculated while passing and hit a truck. Bessie Smith's right arm was partially torn off. A doctor happened to come by and wanted to render aid. But he was himself struck by a car. Bessie Smith was transported by ambulance to G.T. Thomas Hospital in Clarksdale. There her arm was amputated. Nonetheless, she died a few hours later due to internal injuries she had suffered in the crash.

Highway 49 leads from Clarksdale to the capital, Jackson. Joe Williams, who was born in 1903 in Crawford, Mississippi, and died in 1982 in Macon, Mississippi, sang about that highway back in the 1930s. The area around Tutwiler is still the deep and mysterious home of the blues.

> *I got a long tall woman, live on Highway 49*
>
> *You got poor Joe walkin' down, woman, ooh, Lord, Highway 49*
>
> *I'm goin' down Highway 49 border, I'm gonna be rockin' to my head*
>
> *If you ever get the blues, catch the Highway 49!*
>
> *Soon this mornin', boys, I may roll in Jackson town*

"49 Highway Blues"
Big Joe Williams, 1935

Charley Patton's lyrics often center around his own experiences. In "High Sheriff Blues" he describes how he was jailed for being drunk in Belzoni, Mississippi:

> *Get in trouble in Belzoni,*
> > *there ain't no use a-screamin' and cryin'*
> *Mr. Will will take you, back to Belzoni jailhouse flyin'*

"High Sheriff Blues"
Charley Patton, 1934

Patton's "Tom Rushen Blues" tells a similar tale in which Sheriff Tom Day loses his job. The fact that Patton only mentions the names of his protagonists but does not introduce them shows that he wrote and played his songs for a small, local community of listeners who were familiar with those characters and the plots they were involved in.

> *When I woke up, Tom Rushen was shakin' me*
>
> *When you get in trouble, it's no use to screamin'*
> > *and cryin'*
> *Tom Rushen will take you, back to the prison house flyin'*
>
> *It were late one night, Halloway was gone to bed*
> *Mister Day brought whiskey taken from under*
> > *Halloway's head*
>
> *I got up this mornin', Tom Day was standin' 'round*
> *If he lose his office now, he's runnin' from town to town*

"Tom Rushen Blues"
Charley Patton, 1929

Here, everything seems to be about bootleg whiskey. It was not until 1966 that Mississippi abolished prohibition, the last state in the Union. Charley Patton, however, did not live to see this happening. He passed away in Indianola, Mississippi, in 1934.

In the years between 1928 and 1935, the Mississippi Sheiks were the poster boys of music from the Delta. To a large degree, they consisted of the extended Chatmon family with other musicians added on occasion. Their band leader, Henderson Chatmon, had himself been a slave. Their hit "Sitting on Top of the World" was covered by countless blues, ragtime, and skiffle musicians, including Howlin' Wolf.

Another bluesman from the Delta was John Smith Hurt, who made his career as Mississippi John Hurt. He was born in 1892 in Teoc, Mississippi, and died in 1966 in Grenada, Mississippi. This is unusual, because musicians born in the Delta rarely stayed there until they died. It was not easy to make a living there. To make it, they had to move to Chicago like blues guitarists did between the wars and post-World War II, or at least to New Orleans or Memphis, like Elvis Presley had from Tupelo, Mississippi. Just a few older musicians stayed there. Almost all of the younger generation emigrated, primarily to Chicago.

Skip James was born as Nehemiah Curtis James in Yazoo City, Mississippi, in 1902, the same year as Son House, who was born as Eddie James House, Jr. in Riverton, Mississippi. One day, Son House shot a member of his audience at a house party and was sentenced to fifteen years at Parchman Farm. A judge in Clarksdale reopened the case and released House on the condition that he leave Clarksdale. Bukka White, who was born as Booker T.

Washington in 1937, was from Aberdeen, Mississippi. He also shot a man, in 1937. When he became an inmate at Parchman Farm, he already had a fairly brutal reputation. The other prisoners called him "Barrelhouse." Conditions on the prison farm were deplorable at that time. White had it a little bit easier as a musician, because he did not have to do as much hard labor.

> *Judge gimme me life this mornin'*
> *down on Parchman Farm*
>
> *If you wanna do good, you better stay off*
> *old Parchman Farm*
>
> *I'm down on the old Parchman Farm,*
> *but I sho' wanna go back home*

"Parchman Farm Blues"
Bukka White, 1940

Even while he was still imprisoned at Parchman, Bukka White made two recordings for the Library of Congress. Its music ethnologists, John and Alan Lomax, made their most important discoveries in the labor camps of the South. Bob Dylan was also fascinated with Parchman Farm:

> *Baby, please don't go back to New Orleans!*
> *I'm on Parchman Farm, didn't do no wrong*
> *Baby, please don't go back to Jackson town!*

"Baby, Please Don't Go"
traditional / Big Joe Williams /
Version: Bob Dylan, 1962

It is impossible to list all of the exceptional blues musicians from Mississippi. But some of them at least merit mention in addition to those I discuss in more detail: Arthur "Big Boy" Crudup (born 1905 in Forest, Mississippi), Sunnyland Slim (born 1907 in Vance, Mississippi as Albert Luandrew), Howlin' Wolf (born Chester Arthur Burnett 1910 in White Station near West Point, Mississippi), Muddy Waters (aka McKinley Morganfield, born 1913 in Rolling Fork, Mississippi), Willie Dixon (born 1915 as William James Dixon in Vicksburg, Mississippi), John Lee Hooker (born 1917 in Clarksdale, Mississippi), Elmore James (born 1918 as Elmore Brooks in Richland, Mississippi), Albert King (born Albert Nelson in 1923 in Indianola, Mississippi), Jimmy Rogers (aka James A. Lane, born 1924 in Ruleville, Mississippi). In 1925, both Jimmy Reed and B.B. King were born in Mississippi, the former as Mathis James Reed in Dunleith, and the latter as Riley B. King in Berclair; Otis Rush came into the world in 1935 in Philadelphia, Mississippi.

The two most important and influential blues musicians of the first generation grew up in the Delta just a few miles apart: Charley Patton was born in 1891 in Edwards and Robert Johnson arrived a bit later in 1911 as Robert Leroy Dodds in Hazlehurst, Mississippi.

There is no doubt that Robert Johnson is the most influential and most revered blues singer of all time. Not much is known about him, no photo is verified. The one photo that is often used, of a cool man in a hat smoking a cigarette, may well not be Robert Johnson. He left behind 29 recordings. Not much more is known about him, other than that he came from the Mississippi Delta, grew up north of Clarksdale and only lived to the age of 27. You can call him the founding father of the 27 Club. No other musician has had as much influence on popular music as Robert Johnson. Muddy Waters, the Rolling Stones, Eric Clapton: they and many others would not be conceivable but for him.

A cloud of mystery and darkness hung around Johnson. Contemporaries agree, and you can hear it in his recordings. There were always stones in his way and hellhounds on his trail. Shortly before his early death, countless blues singers heard Robert Johnson play, including young Muddy Waters in Clarksdale, the pianist Sunnyland Slim in West Helena and Memphis, David "Honeyboy" Edwards in Itta Bena and other towns. Johnson must have been on the road a lot. In 1938, he was poisoned by his girlfriend in Greenwood, Mississippi, in an act of jealousy. Johnson had a reputation as a passionate and successful ladies' man. But after his death, researchers could not find anyone who knew him in either Clarksdale or San Antonio.

His thin voice is strangely intense and unprecedented. It is eerie and gives listeners a shiver down the spine. His lyrics are thoroughly sinister and full of despair. They are unbelievably suggestive and evocative, and he is an absolute guitar virtuoso. He always seemed haunted by demons. And his lyrics often feature the devil.

This is how the early popular myth got started that Johnson made a deal with the devil. That was the only way to explain how such a burdened and tortured soul could come up with such unique and breathtaking art that seemed so somber and threatening at the same time. Johnson's lyrics gave reason for speculations of this kind when he sang, in "Me and the Devil":

Early this morning, you knocked upon my door

> *I said, "Hello, Satan, I believe, it's time to go."*
> *Me and the devil, both walkin' side by side*
> *You can bury my body down by the highway side*
> *Lord, my old evil spirit can catch a Greyhound bus and ride*

"Me and the Devil"
Robert Johnson, 1937

Legend has it that Robert Johnson met the devil himself at an intersection in Rosedale, about 40 miles southwest of Clarksdale. There, he sold his soul in exchange for becoming a brilliant guitar virtuoso who would be able to express just about anything just playing his guitar.

> *I went to the crossroad, fell down on my knees [...]*
> *You can run, you can run, tell my friend Willie Brown*
> *That I got the crossroad blues this mornin'.*
> *Lord, babe, I am sinkin' down*

"Cross Road Blues"
Robert Johnson, 1936

What is actually known is that Johnson devoted himself intensely to listening to Son House and to Willie Brown, the guitarist mentioned in the above quoted "Cross Road Blues" when he was working and living on Richard Lellman's plantation in Robinsonville. Johnson tried to emulate the musical techniques of both guitar players but found himself incapable of doing so and finally failed tragically. He burnt out from the plantation and vanished for half a year. Then he finally returned, a totally changed man, a guitar virtuoso, and a man adored by women. No wonder the saga of the pact with the devil emerged.

In Clarksdale today, the intersection of US 61 and US 49 has signage that indicates where Johnson allegedly made his deal with the devil. It is a tourist attraction for those who want to discover the dark secrets on the Blues Trail. There are otherwise few sights to see in Mississippi. But the wonderful short film *Beat the Devil* by Tony Scott with James Brown, Clive Owen and Gary Oldman is worth watching.

Egyptian civilization was characterized by periodic flooding of the Nile. That was an agricultural necessity, but it also caused human catastrophe. Things have not been much different in Mississippi. But here, the destruction was in the forefront. And that primarily affected the disadvantaged. Anyone who can afford to do so does not live directly on the river, but rather at a slight elevation so that their houses don't wash away when the water rises. That is why the cities along the Mississippi seem to turn their back on Old Man River unless they are built high up on a ridge.

Many floods have haunted and devastated the land along the river. The worst and most damaging was the Great Mississippi Flood of 1927. After the levees broke, an area of 27,000 square miles, which is about the combined sizes of Vermont, New Hampshire and Massachusetts, was submerged under thirty feet of water. The flood affected 630,000 people, primarily in Arkansas, Louisiana and Mississippi. Many of them were washed away in the flood. The greatest devastation was in the Mississippi Delta. Afterwards, the poor in the Delta lived in tent cities for many years, including 200,000 African Americans, who were the hardest hit. The catastrophe struck a region that was already down and out. The boll weevil, or *Anthomomus grandis*, had wiped out entire harvests for several years prior. And after the floods, the area suffered from equally crippling droughts. And it just kept coming: after Black Friday 1929 on Wall Street, the Great Depression hit the poorest part of the nation extra hard.

The terrible flood contributed to the Great Migration of Black people from the agricultural South to the industrial cities of the Midwest. As a result of the catastrophe of 1927, and the support of F.D. Roosevelt's WPA in the New Deal, the federal government then built the biggest system of flood basins and dams the world had ever seen. But the sprawling agricultural farms and settlements in the Mississippi lowlands now depended on the reliability of the levees:

> *If it keeps on rainin', levee's goin' to break*
> *And the water gonna come in, have no place to stay*
>
> *Cryin' won't help you, prayin' won't do no good*
> *When the levee breaks, mama, you got to lose*

"When the Levee Breaks"
Kansas Joe McCoy (& Memphis Minnie), 1929

This song was written by Joe McCoy immediately after experiencing the Great Mississippi Flood of 1927. It was made popular by Memphis Minnie. Decades later it was covered by Led Zeppelin who added a few interesting verses containing historical reflections on the migration that resulted from the flood that McCoy and Memphis Minnie could not have anticipated:

> *If you're goin' down South*
> *They go no work to do*
>
> *When the levee breaks, mama, you got to move*
>
> *Going, goin' to Chicago*
> *Sorry, but I can't take you*

"When the Levee Breaks"
McCoy/Led Zeppelin, 1971

However, an even more famous blues song about flooding, and its true musical monument, is Charley Patton's "High Water Everywhere":

> *Lord, the whole round country, man,*
>   *is overflowed*
>
> *Look a-here, boys, around Leland tell me,*
>   *river is raging high*
> *I'm going over to Greenville, bought our tickets,*
>   *good-bye!*
>
> *The water at Greenville and Leland, Lord,*
>   *it done rose everywhere*
> *I would go down to Rosedale, but they tell me*
>   *there's water there*
>
> *Back water at Blytheville, done struck Joiner town*
>
> *Oh Lordy, women and children sinking down*
> *I couldn't see nobody home, and was no one to be found*

"High Water Everywhere"
Charley Patton, 1929

This song also has a reincarnation. In the good tradition of oral history and continual riffing off old material, the Nobel laureate, Bob Dylan, wrote a response and update to Charley Patton's song: his "High Water (for Charley Patton)" in 2001. The song is basically an account of the Mississippi flood of 1927, replete with "thunder rolling over Clarksdale" and "water pourin' into Vicksburg". However, Dylan's lyrics are full of references, inside jokes, and quotes that cannot all be explained here. Just a few hints, though: Big Joe Turner was actually born and raised in Kansas City. Bob Dylan makes him a character of Wilbert Harrison, whose hit "Kansas City" originally contained the line "12th Street and Vine". In the Dylan song, "Big Joe Turner [is] lookin' East and West [.] He made it to Kansas City, 12th Street and Vine". But getting there, he realizes there is "nothin' standing there", nothing but "high water everywhere", "coffins droppin' in the street like balloons made out of lead" and "the shacks are slidin' down". There is a reference to the insane protagonist in Charlotte Brontë's novel "Jane Eyre" and a quote from the forgotten blues singer Arthur Blake (1896-1934). God knows where Dylan knew him from. But Dylan is Dylan. And the threads of references and quotations he weaves together, the "hints and allegations" (Paul Simon), carry on the cultural heritage, just because the sources are permanently obliterated, expropriated, recycled and reinvented. Those sources include the cuckoo who "warbles as she flies", and the references to Robert Johnson and "Dust My Broom".

Of course, Mississippi's flood catastrophe hit the poor and disadvantaged disproportionately. Natural disasters make social injustices worse, and not only because it is so hard for the poor to get back on their feet when they are already struggling to survive. Just like after the Katrina catastrophe in New Orleans in 2005, there have been moments of suspicion in Mississippi. Was the failure to render aid part of a conspiracy by the establishment against the rabble of African Americans and White poor crackers that were supposed to be washed away and literally aborted? Randy Newman wrote a beautiful song about this, "Louisiana 1927":

> *The river have busted through,*
>   *clear down to Plaquemines*
> *Six feet of water in the streets of Evangeline*
>
> *Louisiana, Louisiana*
> *They're tryin' to wash us away*
>
> *President say, "Isn't it a shame*
> *What the river has done to this poor cracker's land?"*

"Louisiana 1927"
Randy Newman, 1974

The suspicion that the riffraff should just be washed away and flushed down to the sea is clearly stated here. However, this is not a new idea. Newman is likely pulling from an old blues song published by Robert Hicks from Atlanta immediately after the Mississippi flood of 1927.

> *I was walking down the levee with my head hanging low*
> *Looking for my sweet mama, but she ain't here no mo'*
>
> *I'm sittin' here lookin' at all this mud*

> *My gal got washed away in the Mississippi flood*
>
> *Ain't no women right here, they all got washed away*
> *That's why I'm cryin', Mississippi Heavy Water Blues*

"Mississippi Heavy Water Blues"
Robert Hicks aka Barbecue Bob, 1927

Of course, Mississippi has continued to develop. It probably advanced more in the last two generations than it did in the previous two hundred years. And yet, it is as if time has stood still there. Bob Dylan's breathtakingly beautiful late work "Mississippi" from 2001, may only touch superficially the land along the great river. But it is certainly no coincidence that the state of Mississippi serves as the perfect stage for melancholic resignation.

> *Well, I got here following the Southern Star*
> *I crossed that river just to be where you are*
> *Only one thing I did wrong*
> *Stayed in Mississippi a day too long*

"Mississippi"
Bob Dylan, 2001

CHICAGO

There is a reason we are now going to move from the brutally hot, blazing and unforgiving rural southern backcountry of the Mississippi Delta, to the bitter cold northern metropolis of Chicago: Millions have taken this journey before us. And in the course of this trip they have, more or less as a side effect, invented rock music.

What do you associate with Chicago? The Windy City, broad shoulders, slaughterhouses, organized crime, Bauhaus architecture, Barack Obama? True as all of this may be, isn't it, more than all of this, Chicago rhythm'n'blues—rough, electrified, excited and exciting? That is the seed from which all rock music grew. And the guy who caused it all was the dim-wit German emperor Wilhelm II who willy-nilly drove Europe into the abyss of World War I, thus causing the first major catastrophe of the 20th century. So, what did Crazy Willy do for blues and rock music?

Even without World War I the industrialization of the Western World after the end of the 19th century would have resulted in fewer people working in agriculture in the southern states and more going to the factories of the North.

World War I intensified this trend greatly with the sharp increase in production of armaments. This resulted in an economic boom. It also created increased demand for laborers in the factories once the USA entered the war because many factory workers were drafted and sent to Europe's battlefields.

There had long been an imbalance in wealth between the mostly poor, agrarian South and the wealthy industrial North. Their differing interests in tariffs was one of the contributing factors to the Civil War, along with the issue of slavery. In any case, industrialization, urbanization and the demand for labor in the North as a result of the war caused the largest mass migration in the history of humanity that was not a result of persecution or danger. However, it was to some extent just that, as widespread lynch murders were, of course, perceived by their victims as rather unpleasant.

During the Great Migration, about six million African Americans moved north between 1916 and 1970. Their grandparents or great grandparents had been slaves. Wealthy White Southerners, with their open racist hatred went out of their way to minimize the consequences of the end of slavery and the legal entitlement to equal rights. They made laws whose only intention was to keep down Black citizens. These were called Jim Crow Laws after a cartoonish character in White minstrel shows, usually played by White actors in blackface. Jim Crow was always smiling but dumb as a post, a laughingstock: a slow, infantilized, goofy, and horny creature who could not be emancipated. Jim Crow laws were successful in creating insurmountable hurdles for Blacks. For example, voting rights could be withheld unless a person's grandparents had been allowed to vote, could read and write or held property. For decades such arbitrary decrees excluded former slaves and their descendants from civil rights. For generations Jim Crow laws made it possible to keep the Black population from having a voice and to keep them in misery. Thus, African Americans were kept in bondage even after the formal end of slavery.

So, in their Southern home states African Americans did not have a good life or prospects. The North, however, beckoned with jobs, with significantly less racism, and the bright lights of the big city. Until 1910 more than ninety percent of Black Americans had lived in the South. By the end of the Great Migration only about half remained there, and eighty percent of African Americans lived in cities.

The migration occurred according to a clear pattern. As if they were a group, people from certain rural areas in the South tended to move into certain cities in the North. In the case of Chicago, almost everyone was from Mississippi. No less than half of those who left the state settled down in Chicago.

Big Bill Broonzy, for example, was born in 1893 in Scott, Mississippi, as one of seventeen children. His extended family moved to Arkansas where he grew up and learned a bit of violin. He wanted to become a minister, but mostly worked as a farmer. When a drought bankrupted him in 1916, he worked at a coal mine. The following year, he was drafted. When he was discharged in 1919, he moved to Chicago, found work, and began to play the guitar. After 1932, he finally began to make money cutting records in Chicago. Slowly his reputation grew.

In just twenty years, between 1910 and 1930, the African American population in the North grew by forty percent. However, at the same time there were millions of new immigrants from Europe arriving in the big cities of the

North, mostly from Ireland. Both of these new ethnic groups entered the social ladder on its lowest rung. Necessarily they became competitors for jobs and cheap housing. Tensions quickly arose and in mid-1919 violence erupted that became known as the Red Summer. The most heinous and brutal race riot occurred in Chicago. Many white men had fought in World War I. When they returned after the end of the war in 1918, they were shocked to learn that newly arrived Blacks had taken their jobs at lower wages. In the massacre that followed, thirty-eight people were killed and hundreds injured in Chicago alone.

Despite all odds, the first urban African American culture on US soil emerged in big cities, like Chicago and New York, and soon a black middle class emerged. Bronzeville in Chicago was such a Black middle-class neighborhood. As early as the 1920s it had many African American entrepreneurs. The people of Chicago were proud of their ostentatiously desegregated restaurants. And Chicago blues and rhythm'n'blues had a mixed audience from the very beginning. Much later, albeit after Great Britain, it also had the first white rhythm'n'blues bands, like the Paul Butterfield Blues Band with the incredibly gifted Chicago blues guitarist Mike Bloomfield.

These developments had enormous ramifications on the development of the music of the 20th century. As already mentioned, Chicago became home to a very large number of Blacks from rural Mississippi. And most of them came from the impoverished Delta. Poverty and discrimination were unbearable there. But the Delta was also the cradle of the blues, particularly of acoustic country and folk blues. Among the many musicians who migrated North from the Delta were Muddy Waters, Chester Burnett (Howlin' Wolf) and Eddie Boyd. Nowhere else could you find such a concentration of exceptional blues musicians.

> *New York is loaded with people*
> *Papers is all loaded with news*
> *L.A. is loaded with movie stars*
> *But Chicago is loaded with the blues*
>
> *We got blues that'll make you lonesome*
> *We got blues that'll make you sad*
> *We got blues that'll make you happy*

"Chicago Is Loaded with the Blues"
Clifton James, 1972

Chicago, with its race wars and high crime rate, was not exactly a paradise. But it was still better than the hell made of poverty and segregation down in Mississippi:

> *Nothing I got 'gainst Mississippi*
> *It also was the home of my wife*
> *But I count myself a lucky man*
> *Just to get away with my life*
>
> *Down in Mississippi where I was born*
> *Down in Mississippi where I come from*
>
> *They had a huntin' season on a rabbit*
> *If you shoot him, you went to jail*
> *The season was always open on me*
> *Nobody needed no bail*

"Down in Mississippi"
J.B. Lenoir, 1966

After its arrival in Chicago, the blues became hard, shrill, and loud. The slow and tender music, for instance of a Mississippi John Hurt from the rural Delta, was worlds apart from the raging storm produced on stage by the likes of Muddy Waters, Howlin' Wolf, T-Bone Walker or Elmore James. It was no longer the same music, but it still had the same structure: twelve or eight bars with the same chords and three-line verses.

Like every cultural revolution, the electrification of Chicago blues, and especially Chicago rhythm'n'blues, the louder and more aggressive cousin of the Delta blues, happened because social, technological and commercial reasons aligned. Now more Black musicians than before could make a living from their music. No longer were they cotton pickers or hired hands for whom playing music in local joints was a side hustle. Also, they didn't have to travel extensively. In a metropolis like Chicago, they catered to an audience of millions who had money in their pockets from their factory jobs. They were also homesick for the Old South, its food and its music. By the way, this explains why the city of Chicago is hardly ever mentioned in Chicago blues. The whole point was to cater to the yearning for the place they had left behind and hated and longed for at the same time. It was as if for one night they would return home, if only through the music.

However, the musicians no longer plucked away on an acoustic guitar amongst a dozen of their friends in a rural barn. Now they performed in large concert halls and on stages that granted them an income sufficient for them to give up their day jobs. On the other hand, the new settings brought about technical and acoustic challenges. Since 1925 it had been possible to amplify guitars. The new aggressive, distorted and overdriven sound began as a technical flaw, but soon it became very popular and was used as a stylistic means of this new urban and modern music. It went well with the wailing or outright threatening character of the lyrics in this urban form of the blues.

However, the migrants from the rural South, who suddenly found themselves in the cold, hectic metropolis with its very different customs, could not always cope with their new surroundings. They generally had not moved North with many possessions, but they brought cultural baggage of lifestyle habits and manners. In the modern city, this seemed quaint and inappropriate. Many a relationship failed because of it. Usually, it was a younger man who migrated first. He first looked for work and modest accommodation. And then he called for his girlfriend, fiancée or wife. Countless songs of the time tell the tale of how the big city went straight to the heads of these young women and how they ran into moral conflicts with their traditional values, but primarily with their men. But of course, it was mostly the men who could not stand to see their down-home women step out into emancipated city life.

> *Bright lights, big city gone to my baby's head*
> *I'm tryin' to tell the woman,*
> *but she don't believe a thing I said*

> "Bright Lights, Big City"
> Jimmy Reed, 1961

Things didn't always end well, and many songs thematize the threat of a young man to send his woman back to their provincial old place in the South:

> *Well, your momma and your daddy told me, baby*
> *Not to take you from the South*
> *I took you to the city when you were a child*
> *And the fight 'bout knocked you out [...]*

> *Well, you run the streets with your wig hair, trying to*
>   *play your high-class games*
> *You run the streets both day and night,*
>   *you don't have pocket change*
>
> *Well, I just can't understand it, baby*
> *What is that makes your head so hot, what is it?*
> *I'm gonna take you back to Georgia,*
>   *right back where you belong, yes I am*

"Gonna Send You Back to Georgia"
B.J. Thomas, 1966

There were endless variations on this theme:

> *Yeah, I'm gonna send you back to Georgia,*
>   *honey that's where you belong*
> *Hang around here, baby,*
>   *and break up my happy home*
>
> *"Goodbye, little woman" is all I have to say.*
> *Give me back what I brought you*
>   *and be on your merry way*

"Gonna Send You Back to Georgia"
James Carr, 1968

Or short and sweet:

> *Tell your mama, tell your pa*
> *I'm gonna send you back to Arkansas*
> *Oh yes, if you don't do right, don't do right*

"What'd I Say"
Ray Charles, 1959

And, of course, there were cases where it was the woman who threatened to return to the South, but her man pleaded with her to stay:

> *Baby, please don't go*
> *Back to New Orleans!*
> *You know it hurt me so*

"Baby, Please Don't Go,"
Big Joe Williams, 1935

From the 1920s to 1960s, you could make a lot of money playing the blues in Black magnet cites like Chicago, New York, Cleveland or Detroit, not only with concerts and in night clubs, but also increasingly through record sales. That was not only because their sound quality had improved, but also because of the increasing wealth of the growing middle class.

In 1950, the Polish Jewish immigrants, Leonard and Phil Chess, founded Chess Records in Chicago. It developed into the most important and influential record label for blues and rhythm'n'blues. At first, the brothers ran two studios. The one at 2120 South Michigan Avenue became a legend. Today, it is home to Willie Dixon's Blues Heaven Foundation. Dixon was Chess's producer, composer and bassist. He probably wrote more blues hits than anybody else.

Bo Diddley, Buddy Guy, Otis Rush, Muddy Waters, Junior Wells, Sonny Boy Williamson and Howlin' Wolf were all among the stars of Chess Records. In the mid-1960s, the studio moved to 320 East 21st Street, before it was given up in 1975. Its catalogue became part of the Universal library.

The fact that the blues had turned into an industry led not only to higher sales numbers, faster beats and screaming guitars. It also made the producers look for female singers, women who could stand their ground on stage and in the record store. Initially, the blues had been a very masculine phenomenon. Almost all country blues singers were men, their lyrics were written from a masculine perspective. They viewed the world from a male point of view and commented on it for a male audience. In a way, it was implicitly assumed that women did not have the blues. But now, suddenly, there was demand for female blues singers, among them the incomparable Bessie Smith. In 1923, she excelled with a song about a huge fire in Chicago, most likely the catastrophe of 1871, in which most of Chicago's inner city vanished. One third of the city's population became homeless, and three hundred died:

> *Late last night, I stole away and cried*
> *Late last night, I stole away and cried*
> *Had the blues for Chicago and I just can't be satisfied*
>
> *Blues on my brain, my tongue refused to talk*
> *Blues on my brain, my tongue refused to talk*
> *I was followin' my daddy, but my feet refuses to walk*
>
> *Mean old fireman, cruel old engineer*
> *Lord, mean old fireman, cruel old engineer*
> *You took my man away and left his mama standing here*
>
> *Big red headline, tomorrow Defender news*
> *Big red headline, tomorrow Defender news*
> *"Woman dead down home," these old Chicago blues*
> *I said blues*

"Chicago Bound Blues"
Bessie Smith, 1923

This new kind of blues brought about specialized lyricists who wrote for female singers and their male audiences. The whole point was to come up with texts as ambiguous and lascivious as possible. Here, a few examples from the mid-1920s:

> *Just like Anne, long and slim,*
>   *when she whip it, it's too bad for Jim, Lord*
> *She whip it to a jelly and stir it in a bowl*
> *Now you whip it to a jelly, if you like good jelly roll*
> *I wear my skirt up to my knee,*
>   *and whip that jelly with who I please*

"Whip It to a Jelly"
Clara Smith, 1926

Or:

> *A Ford is a car everybody wants to ride*
> *Jump in, you will see!*
> *You can all have a Rolls-Royce, a Packard and such*
> *It takes a Ford engine, boys, to do your stuff*
> *I've got Ford engine movements in my hips*
> *Ten thousand miles guaranteed*

"I've Got Ford Movement in My Hips"
Cleo Gibson, 1929

The car metaphor was immensely popular. It allowed for countless jokes. Also, the booming automobile industry had become the biggest employer for Blacks in the North. In song, sexual problems were narrated in images of malfunctioning cars. You can find that in Lightnin' Hopkins's little tune, "My Starter Won't Start this Morning". It is a song about bad women and bad fuel.

> *My starter won't start this mornin'*
> *Boy, and my motor won't even turn*
> *You know, I've been runnin' with a fast, trashy womens*
> *Now, they'll call my little car to ruin*
>
> *Mechanic say "Your car's all right like*
> *You just been burnin' bad gasoline."*

"My Starter Won't Start this Morning"
Lightnin' Hopkins, 1969

Another example is Wilson Pickett's "Mustang Sally":

> *I bought you a brand-new Mustang,*
>   *a nineteen sixty-five*
> *Now you come around signifying, woman,*
>   *you don't want to let me ride*

"Mustang Sally"
Wilson Pickett, 1966

And there's even "Start Me Up" by The Rolling Stones:

> *If you start it up*
> *Kick on the starter give it all you got, you got, you got!*
> *I can't compete with the riders in the other heats [...]*
>
> *My eyes dilate, my lips go green*
> *My hands are greasy, she's a mean, mean machine*

"Start Me Up"
The Rolling Stones, 1981

"Me and My Chauffeur Blues" exemplifies an interesting mix of social and sexual emancipation, fascination with cars and unrealistic fantasies of upward mobility:

Won't you be my chauffeur, won't you be my chauffeur?
I wants him to drive me, I wants him to drive me
　downtown
Yes he drives so easy, I can't turn him down

But I don't want him, but I don't want him
To be ridin' these girls, to be ridin' these girls around
So, I'm gonna steal me a pistol, shoot my chauffeur down

Well, I must buy him, well, I must buy him
A brand new V8, a brand new V8 Ford
Then he won't need no passengers, I will be his load

Going to let my chauffeur, going to let my chauffeur
Drive me around the, drive me around the world
Then he can be my little boy, yes, I'll be his girl.

"Me and My Chauffeur Blues"
Memphis Minnie, 1941

"Me and My Chauffeur Blues" was Memphis Minnie's greatest success. She is a good example of Chicago's blues singers, especially female singers, of the first generation. Born in 1897, in a suburb of New Orleans, she moved with her parents to Memphis when she was seven. Later, they moved on farther north, to Chicago.

The Old South, unfaithful women or men, sex, alcohol and cars—those were the subjects of the Chicago blues. But it also celebrated a newly-won self-consciousness and pride. No longer would Blacks be despised, humiliated and addressed as "boys." Now they acted as sexually confident men, as emancipated and self-reliant members of the middle class. It should come as no surprise that these topics resonated with pubescent, White, pimply-faced rhythm'n'blues fans of the 1960s and 1970s.

> *I'm a man*
> *I spell: "M"*
> *"A", child*
> *"N"*
> *That represent "man"*
> *No "B"*
> *"O", child*
> *"Y"*
>
> *That spell "mannish boy"*
> *I'm a man*
> *I'm a full-grown man*

"Mannish Boy"
Muddy Waters, 1955

As a rule, the legal, social and sexual emancipation were one:

> *All you pretty women*
> *Standin' in line*
> *I can make love to you, baby*
> *In an hour's time*
>
> *I'm a man*
> *I spell "M-A-N"*
>
> *Goin' back down*
> *To Kansas town*
> *To bring back the second cousin*
> *Little Johnny the Conqueroo*

"I'm a Man"
Bo Diddley, 1955

John the Conqueror is a mythical hero in African American folklore who was able to outsmart his slave holder. This character and his name can be traced from Chicago to the Mississippi Delta and via New Orleans and the Caribbean to what is, today, Ghana. There he was called John Carney, in Jamaica John Canoe, Creole Junkarooacome, which probably is the root of the mysterious but omnipresent Jock-a-mo in New Orleans slang.

One year before Bo Diddley recorded, "I'm a Man", Muddy Waters sang:

> *I got John the Conqueror*
> *I'm gonna mess with you*

"Hoochie Coochie Man"
Willie Dixon, 1954

John the Conqueror is also called Conqueroo, which is an abbreviation of its namesake plant, John the Conqueror Root, either *Alpina galanga* or *Trillium grandiflorum* depending on taste or the intended effect. It was supposed to evoke magical powers, including, but not only, of the sexual kind. You better didn't mess or compete with Muddy Waters. Wikipedia says that the root is, "used as one of the parts of a mojo bag. It is typically used in sexual spells of various sorts, and it is also considered lucky for gambling. It is likely that the root acquired its sexual magical reputation because, when dried, it resembles the testicles of a dark-skinned man."

Interesting...

Like all new homes, Chicago has been hated and idolized at the same time. Of course, the terrible cold in the proverbial Windy City is the subject of song:

> *Well, the winds in Chicago*

> *have turned me to shreds…*

Cold Irons Bound,
Bob Dylan, 1997

The city's cold and roughness are what makes Chicago Chicago:

> *Let's leave Chicago to the Eskimos!*
> *That town's a little bit too rugged*

"I Love L.A."
Randy Newman, 1983

There is no shortage of complaints about both. The city is famous for its violence. For many years organized crime, the Mob, controlled the city:

> *Well, the Southside of Chicago*
> *Is the baddest part of town*
> *And if you go down there*
> *You better just beware*
> *Of a man named Leroy Brown [...]*
>
> *Now, Leroy he a gambler*
> *And he like his fancy clothes*
> *And he like to wave his diamond rings*
> *In front of everybody's nose*
>
> *He got a thirty-two gun in his pocket for fun*
> *He got a razor in his shoe*

"Bad, Bad Leroy Brown"
Jim Croce, 1972

Even today the murder rate in Chicago is almost four

times as high as the national average. However, it is mainly Black youths dying nowadays. The dead are no longer members of Al Capone's mafia organization called the Chicago Outfit. Now they die as bystanders who were at the wrong place at the wrong time, as petty criminals or members of rival drug gangs:

> *As the snow flies*
> *On a cold and grey Chicago mornin'*
> *A poor little baby child is born*
> *In the ghetto*

The little boy grows up hungry:

> *So, he starts to roam the streets at night*
> *And he learns how to steal, and he learns how to fight*
> *In the ghetto*

Finally, he dies in a botched car theft:

> *And as the young man dies*
> *On a cold and grey Chicago mornin'*
> *Another little baby child is born*
> *In the ghetto*

"In the Ghetto"
Elvis Presley, 1969

"In the Ghetto" was really a weak platitude of social kitsch, a late work by a worn-out 34-year-old Elvis. The true voice of Black misery, of coming change and of the civil rights movement, had long been Curtis Mayfield, at least after he wrote the 1965 anthem "People Get Ready". He was born in Chicago in 1942 and grew up in the projects of Cabrini-Green. But if you were asked to think of *one* song about Chicago, you would not think of "In the Ghetto", nor of "People Get Ready", but of "Sweet Home Chicago".

This song has become iconic for Chicago, just like "New York, New York" for New York City or "Georgia on My Mind" for Georgia. Robert Johnson, however, its most likely author and the first performer known to sing the song, probably did not even write it about Chicago, Illinois. Instead, what has since become the anthem of the Windy City was probably about a rather insignificant place called Port Chicago in California. The first lyrics from 1936 are:

> *Oh baby, don't you want to go?*
> *Back to the land of California,*
> *to my sweet home Chicago*

"Sweet Home Chicago"
Robert Johnson, 1936

Did Johnson simply not know his geography? That seems unlikely as he makes no mistakes in any of his twenty-nine recorded songs. It is probably as simple as that: The song is about another Chicago, Port Chicago in California. In order to turn it into the anthem of the Second City, the song needed a slight tweak. In his 2004 version, Eric Clapton tried his hand:

> *Come on, baby don't you wanna go?*
> *Back from the land of California to my*
> *sweet home Chicago*

"Sweet Home Chicago"
Johnson/Clapton, 2004

Later he decided to get rid of "California" altogether. He simply went back to Freddie King's version from the seventies:

> *Come on, baby don't you want to go*
> *To the same old place, sweet home Chicago [...]*
>
> *I'm goin' to Chicago, two thousand miles away*

"Sweet Home Chicago"
Johnson/King, 1974

After all, the people of Chicago needed an anthem of their own, and you had to deliver.

It worked. Since the 1960s, thousands of Chicagoans have belted out the song in bars and at sports events on a regular basis. At the same time, blues fans and researchers involved themselves in much controversy about the meaning of Robert Johnson's original lines. Strange interpretations made the rounds, among them that the song was about a tour across the USA. There was also a bizarre theory that Robert Johnson has created a man, the first-person narrator, a cheat and scoundrel, or maybe just a total idiot. That man is trying to lure a woman to a place that does not exist.

There is an obvious fascination with places and landscapes in this music. And the Great Migration exemplifies unprecedented mobility. Modern urban life after World War I, and especially the car industry and the highway system that shaped the nation at this time, are reflected in the lyrics of the time. The nascent self-confidence of the new Black middle class and its growing wealth are mirrored in songs about both romantic relationships and automobility.

I'm goin' to Chicago;
 that's the last place my baby stayed
I'm packin' up my bags,
 I'm gonna leave this old town right away

"Chicago City",
 that's what the sign on the highway read
I'm gonna keep on movin'
 'til I get to that street corner 6th and Main
I've got to find that girl,
 if I have to hitch hike 'round the world

"Hitch Hike"
Marvin Gaye, 1962

I have been to Chicago six times and find the city exceedingly beautiful, if not a bit cold for my taste and certainly very windy. I'm goin' to Chicago, if I have to hitch hike 'round the world.

MAP OF
TEXAS

TEXAS

There's a place not too far away from here
Well, they call it Texas, and it's a mighty fine place to be

Runs from Texarkana to El Paso
And there's Houston, Dallas, Austin and San Antone
People in Texas sure do make you feel at home

"Texas"
Charlie Daniels, 1975

Texas is a world unto itself. The first time I travelled there, I entered from Mexico. It was 1983 and I had just criss-crossed Mexico by bus. We were students weighed down by bulky backpacks and looking pretty road weary. Friendly Mexican fellow passengers had been very generous to me and my girlfriend. We enjoyed gifts of bread, homemade cheese, nuts and Mexican salsa. We walked across the border from Ciudad Juárez to El Paso. An imposing immigration officer asked us if we had any food with us. Although I knew it was prohibited to bring in consumables,

I answered in the affirmative. The man, in his broad-brimmed hat, mirrored sunglasses and uniform, said in his inimitable drawl, "This is Texas, Son." And then he waved us through.

I was fascinated. Not so much by his strange, ambiguous response, but more by the fact that his face showed no expression and that he could speak while his top teeth remained in close contact with his lower incisors. I continued on my way to the Promised Land of Texas with a, "thank you, Sir." And that was the first and last time I ever addressed anyone as "Sir".

On this trip, we went to strange places riding on *Tres Estrellas* and Greyhound buses. If you went to these places as a tourist today, you wouldn't survive. I remember Van Horn, Texas, because I wrote a song about it later that my band still plays sometimes. Van Horn consists of a gas station, a couple of ramshackle trailer homes and a few houses. Desert sand blows between them. It's the Texas Europeans dream of. But it's surprising how much water and how many rivers actually flow through the real Texas. One needs a rhyme to make reason of them all:

> *We crossed the wild Pecos*
> *We forded the Nueces*
> *We swum the Guadalupe*
> *We followed the Brazos*
> *Red River runs rusty*
> *The Wichita clear*
> *But down by the Brazos*
> *I courted my dear*
>
> *The fair Angelina*
> *Runs glossy and gliding*
> *The crooked Colorado*

Runs weaving and winding
The slow San Antonio
It courses the plains
But I never will walk
By the Brazos again

The Trinity's muddy
And the Brazos quicksandy

The girls of Little River
They're plump and they're pretty
The Sabine and the Sulphur
Have many a beauty
On the banks of the Neches
There's girls by the score
But down by the Brazos
I'll wander no more

There's many a river
That waters the land

"The Texas River Song"
aka. "The Brazos River"
traditional

When you think of music from Texas, your first association will most likely be country & western. Like most generalizations and clichés, this one is false and correct at the same time. First of all, there are and have been for a long time many other styles and strands of popular and folk music in Texas: blues, bluegrass, folk, funk, gospel, jazz, norteña, polkas, rock'n'roll, soul, tejano conjunto, waltzes and many more. But the other issue with the term "country & western" is that it implies a merger, an amalgam whilst the truth looks more like a salad in a bowl: Country music is almost exclusively based on European folk traditions and church hymns, mostly from England, Germany, Ireland and Scotland. In traditional country music, like in a Hank Williams song, you will hardly ever find more than four chords, and rarely more harmonic sophistication than a seventh chord. The "western" element in "country & western", however, does contain a lot of Central European song structures, like polkas, waltzes, schottische, ländler and so on. But it is played in an unmistakably swinging way. That is why it has also been called "western swing". It is, despite the origin of its song structures, jazz. And there are very rare moments when the twain did ever meet, like in a few songs by the likes of Lyle Lovett or, of course, in zydeco. Generally speaking, it is a safe assumption that country and western music sounds *either* country *or* western.

Like in almost all popular music in North America, however, there is virtually always an African element in it. Even "pure" White singers like Buck Owens or Hank Snow had that, although they may not even have been aware of it. But after all, they did not sound European. The most striking example of creative misunderstandings and fruitful fusion, however, may be the history of yodeling in Texas.

Yes, yodeling.

When it comes to yodeling, most people don't think of Africa. Sometimes so-called "blue yodeling" sounds irritating to people from the Alpine countries, like me. But yodeling in Texas did not have its roots in Central Europe. Its origins were African Americans who traveled through the country with snake oil or minstrel shows. The songs they yodeled to can be considered precursors of the blues. In the 1920s and 1930s, yodeling became so popular that there were even different styles. Experts differentiate between the "archaic yodeler of the 19th century," and the "fake blue yodel." Because Texas yodeling was predominantly Black in the beginning and not associated with Europe, White yodelers were sometimes called "White men gone Black." Texan yodelers were called "Swiss yodelers with Black content." In the late 1920s, yodeling went more mainstream as "pop country yodel" and was commercially successful. It was this subgenre in which Jimmy Long excelled with "Yodel Your Troubles Away", his 1929 hit. The big breakthrough, however, came with "T for Texas". It put yodeling in the heart of Texans and was a huge smash hit for Jimmie Rodgers in February of 1928.

> *T for Texas, T for Tennessee*
> *T for Thelma*
> *That gal that made a wreck out of me*

"T for Texas"
Jimmie Rodgers, 1928

The yodeling trend that Rodgers started in Texas produced many copycats and kicked off a yodeling craze. Ernest Tubb, for example, who was born on a cotton farm in Crisp, Texas, in 1914, and later moved to San Antonio, was inspired to yodel by listening to Jimmie Rodgers recordings. And Don Walser, who was born in 1934 in Brownfield, Texas, and died in Austin, may be called the last traditional yodeler of Texas. But Walser did not just yodel. At the age of sixteen he founded his first band together with Buddy Holly, The Panhandle Playboys. Yodeling and rock 'n' roll came together. Later, Walser founded the Texas Plainsmen.

Texas, in the imagination of Texans, is still filled with cattle punchers, card sharks, gunslingers and rodeo riders. The highway to Amarillo, for instance, still seems to be the epitome of freedom for them:

> *Well, I'm a high straight in Plainview*
> *Side bet in Idalou*
> *And a fresh deck in New Deal*
> *I don't wear no Stetson*
> *But I'm willin' to bet, son*
> *That I'm a big a Texan as you are*
>
> *And close I'll ever get to heaven*
> *Is makin' speed up ol' 87*
> *Of that hard-ass Amarillo highway*

"Amarillo Highway"
Terry Allen, 1993

There are a lot of movies that place those lonesome heroes in the midst of a modern city skyline. Films like John Huston's *Misfits* (1961), John Schlesinger's *Midnight Cowboy* (1969), Sam Peckinpah's *The Wild Bunch* (1969) and *Pat Garrett and Billy the Kid* (1973), even Sydney Pollack's *The Electric Horseman* (1979) and James Bridges's *Urban Cowboy* (1980) deconstruct the cowboy as a miserable, broken character, out of time and out of touch with the changed world around him. These cowboys who stubbornly cling to old notions of freedom try to make a living as rodeo riders or simply drink themselves to death. But they are still around, the cowboys, gamblers, and the old warhorses traveling from one rodeo to the next. Larry Gatlin, too, likes to think of himself as a rodeo professional, but he really is a singer who stays in Holiday Inns. This is what has become of the West that once was wild:

> *Oh, honey, Houston*
> *Houston means the last day of the tour and we're*
> *through [...]*
>
> *And sleepin' all alone in that Holiday Hotel*
> *Sure makes a cowboy blue*
>
> "Houston (Means I'm One Day Closer to You)"
Larry Gatlin, 1983

But of course, the classic song about Houston was performed by Dean Martin replete with Stetson and cigarette. In this song, written by Lee Hazlewood in 1964, the first-person narrator yearns for Houston and his girl there:

> *Well, it's lonesome in this old town*
> *Everybody puts me down*
>
> *I got a girl waiting out for me*
> *Well, at least she said she'd be*
> *Going back to Houston, Houston, Houston*
>
> "Houston"
Lee Hazlewood, 1964

Dylan's Houston is also a place of longing, but in the tradition of the blues. A vagabond warns his kith and kin of overly zealous sheriffs and a "man with the shining star":

> *If you ever go to Houston, boy, you better walk right*
> *If you're ever down there on Bagby and Lamar*
> *You better watch out for the man with the shining star*
> *Better know where you're going or stay where you are*
>
> "If You Ever Go to Houston"
Bob Dylan, 2009

Here Dylan is referring to a traditional prison song, "Midnight Special", recorded by Leadbelly in 1934 and which calls out a sheriff by name:

> *If you ever go to Houston, oh you better walk right*
> *And you better not wobble, and you better not fight*
> *Sheriff Rocko will arrest you,*
>   *Eddie Boone will take you down*
> *You can bet your bottom dollar,*
>   *you're Sugarland bound*

"Midnight Special"
traditional/Leadbelly 1934

It seems Sheriff Rocko had it in for vagrants and drunks.

Another important town and subject in Texas is "San Antone"—or San Antonio. This was once the center of the German settlement of Texas. It is not only where the inmates of Johnny Cash's "Folsom Prison" want to be. Since 1938, when Bob Wills and His Texas Playboys recorded "San Antonio Rose", San Antonio has represented what is beautiful in and about Texas. However, it also stands for the Alamo, a fort where more than two hundred Texans died in the 1836 battle of the Texas Revolution that later became so crucial for Texan pride:

> *Deep within my heart lies a melody*
> *A song of old San Antone*
> *It was there I found beside the Alamo*
> *Enchantment strange as the blue up above*
> *Call back my rose, rose of San Antone!*

"New San Antonio Rose"
Bob Wills and His Texas Playboys, 1940

Bob Dylan, on the other hand, has rendered a kind of imaginary western fantasy movie wherein the Alamo and San Antonio are identified with a love story and restless wandering (though, it was Sam Shepard who wrote the lyrics for this song):

> *Well, we drove that car all night into San Antone*
> *And we slept near the Alamo, your skin was so tender and soft*

> "Brownsville Girl"
> Bob Dylan and Sam Shepard, 1986

Then there's the town of El Paso made famous by an old ballad of love, jealousy, and murder:

> *Out in the West Texas town of El Paso*
> *I fell in love with a Mexican girl*
> *Night time would find me in Rosa's cantina [...]*
> *One night a wild young cowboy came in*
> *Wild as the West Texas wind*

Raging with jealousy, the protagonist shoots and kills the handsome stranger, steals a horse and rides...

> *Just as fast as I could from the West Texas town*
>   *of El Paso*
> *Out to the badlands of New Mexico*

Finally admitting...

> *Back in El Paso my life would be worthless...*

> "El Paso"
> Marty Robbins, 1959

There follow a few more verses that tell of the foreseeable and tragic end to this tale with the lovely Mexican girl cradling her dying lover. Because even gunslinging, roughshod Texans, as they like to think of themselves, seem to know love. At some point, every weary hobo or cowboy wants to settle down when he finds his Texas beauty.

Here is the story of a young guy from Louisiana who, having "got the ramblin' fever," rides across the state line into Texas and ends up in Austin ("just ask any cowboy, he'll tell you it's the best"). What happens next?

> *I met a Texas beauty I got friendly with her pa*
> *I looked in to her big blue eyes this is what I saw*
> *Miles of Texas [...]*
> *I saw miles and miles of Texas,*
> *Gonna live here till I die*

"Miles and Miles of Texas"
Tommy Camfield and Diane Johnston, 1961

Folklore and pop music make the love affair of Texans with Texas abundantly clear. In the very beginning, at the origin of Texan love songs, this still sounded rather unsophisticated and a bit naïve. In the early 19th century for instance, love sounded like this in Texas:

> *There's a yellow rose in Texas*
> *That I am goin' back to see*
> *Nobody else could miss her*
> *Not half as much as me*
> *She cried so when I left her*
> *It like to broke my heart*
> *And if I ever find her*
> *We never more will part*

> *She's the sweetest little rosebud*
> *That Texas ever knew*
> *Her eyes are bright as diamonds*
> *They sparkle like the dew*
> *You may talk about your Clementine*
> *And sing of Rosa Lee*
> *But the Yellow Rose of Texas*
> *Is the only girl for me*
>
> "The Yellow Rose of Texas"
> J.K./traditional, early 19th century

This is how things were. This is the sound of the 19th century. During the Civil War, this song rose to great fame as it was sung by soldiers on both sides of the conflict to the drums of a military band while they were butchering each other to death. But today everything is maybe even more complicated.

If you take a closer look, love songs about Texas are not really love songs. They are songs about paradise lost, full of reminiscences and longing and always sung from a distance. This pain of separation that gives rise to the lyrics, isn't it more often about the land? Isn't the one the singer is longing for, his beloved, isn't that really Texas itself? The loved one, Texas, and the singer himself, aren't they one and the same? Everything blends into one longing, into a state of Texas. By the way, Texas has eyes and it lives in the singer:

> *For the girls I've known in San Antone*
> *And out El Paso way*
> *My love grows like a yellow rose [...]*
>
> *I'm livin' in a state of Texas*
> *And Texas lives in me [...]*

The eyes of Texas are smiling on me

"A State of Texas"
Old 97's, 2010

In general, country music has an erotic relationship with Texas. It enjoys the pain of longing. In "Waltz Across Texas" the state is claimed by dancing across it, like the first White settlers staked their claims, or just like half-crazy Travis in Wim Wender's blood-and-soil film, "Paris, Texas", who paces off his ridiculous plot in the desert:

> *When we dance together, my world's in disguise*
> *It's a fairyland tale that come true*
> *And when you look at me with those stars in your eyes*
> *I could waltz across Texas with you*

"Waltz Across Texas"
Ernest Tubb, 1965

You can take two-step lessons on YouTube set to "Waltz Across Texas".

The "Texas State of Mind" is as ambiguous as Billy Joel's famous "New York State of Mind", albeit totally different. While Joel plays with the meanings of "mental condition" and "republic of intellectuals" in 1976, David Frizzell's 1981 Texan reply is based on the double meaning of a love between two people and that of Texas as a country. (I have marked the text with DF for David Frizzell and SW for Shelly West):

> *DF:*
> *California's too damn far from you and that*
>   *old Lone Star*

> *SW:*
> *I need to hold you again, so come home*
> *While you're in a Texas state of mind!*

"Texas State of Mind"
Cliff Crofford, John Durrill
and Snuff Garrett, 1981

There was a reply to this song, too. In 1987, Nanci Griffith recorded the really rather beautiful love song "Lone Star State of Mind". The Lone Star has already been mentioned in "Texas State of Mind", as well as the division between Texas and Colorado or California. But "Lone Star State of Mind" clearly belongs in the sub-genre of songs of reminiscence and longing.

> *Your phone call took me by surprise*
> *Gee, it's been a long, long time*
> *Since those hot and humid Texas nights*
> *When we went swimm'n in the tide*
> *Corpus Christi seems so far away*
> *I'm in a Lone Star state of mind*

"Lone Star State of Mind"
Fred Koller, Patrick Alger and
Gene Levine for Nanci Griffith, 1987

The same thing goes for "I Wish It Would Rain", also by Nanci Griffith:

> *I'm gonna pack up my two-step shoes and head*
>   *for the Gulf Coast Plains*
> *I want to walk the streets of my own hometown*
>   *where everybody knows my name*
> *I want to ride a ways down to Galveston...*

Cause that Gulf Coast water tastes as sweet as wine

"I Wish It Would Rain"
Nanci Griffith, 1988

There is some similarity with the song "Galveston", released by Glen Campbell in 1969. Like "Lone Star State of Mind", it is about the memory of swimming together in the Gulf of Mexico a long time ago. This time, however, the fear of dying is blended with the pain from what has been lost. The first-person narrator seems to be a soldier in Vietnam:

Galveston, oh, Galveston
I still hear your sea winds blowing
I still see her dark eyes glowing

I clean my gun, and dream of Galveston
And is she waiting there for me
On the beach where we used to run?

Galveston, I am so afraid of dying

"Galveston"
Jimmy Webb, 1969

Love songs from Texas are love songs about Texas. They deal with loss and insatiable longing. They are always in soft focus and backlit, putting everything else in their shadow.

That lonesome Texas sun was setting so low
And in the rear-view mirror I watched it go
I can still see the wind in her golden hair

> *I close my eyes for a moment, I'm still here*
> *The bluest eyes in Texas*
> *Are haunting me tonight*

"The Bluest Eyes in Texas"
Tim DuBois, Dave Robbins and Van Stephenson
for Restless Heart, 1988

Always, things have gone wrong before the song even begins. Love in Texas seems to be a memory, a nocturnal fiction. Not even Fort Worth beer can help. (Perhaps good old George Strait should have tried Shiner Bock by Spötzl Brewery in Shiner, Texas instead. It's in a class of its own.)

> *Cold Fort Worth beer just ain't no good for jealous*
> *I try it night after night...*
>
> *You left me here to be with him in Dallas*
> *Does Fort Worth ever cross your mind?*

"Does Fort Worth Ever Cross Your Mind"
Sanger D. Shafer and Darlene Shafer
for George Strait, 1984

This is what happens when you drink the wrong beer. I can't really sympathize with that. It becomes clear: Only in a very few cases does the singer beg his faraway loved one to come back to him. If not for his sake, or because of the good relationship they once had, the pretext is simple. Of course, it is not because the singer wants his girl back. Instead, it is for the good of Texas and to make sure she doesn't lose her beautiful accent. In "Come Back to Texas", he doesn't even try to lure her back by declaring his love for her. Instead, he claims she is missed by NASA and a famous professional football player:

> *So, when you're done doing whatever*
> *And when you're through doing whoever*
> *You know Denton County will be right here*
> *   waiting for you*
> *Come back to Texas!*
>
> *Before you lose your accent*
> *And forget all about the Lone Star State*
> *Troy Aikman wants you back*
> *NASA wants you back*

"Ohio (Come Back to Texas)"
Bowling for Soup, 2004

And even if it is not paradise, Texas must be the place where angels dare to dwell:

> *If you want to see heaven, brother, here's your chance*
> *I've been sent to spread the message:*
> *God blessed Texas*

"God Blessed Texas"
Porter Howell, Brady Seals, 1993

Pat Green and Lyle Lovett assumed the task of describing these celestial beings in more detail. Also, they tried to implement benchmarking standards by praising the virtues of women in other states but concluding that:

> *If you can find a Lone Star gal, boy, you better get 'r*
> *Once you cross that Red River, hoss*
> *You'll stay there forever*
> *'Cause the girls in Texas are just a little bit better*

"Girls from Texas"
Jon Randall and Shane L. McAnally, 2015

This special quality of Texas, however, can also backfire. Anyone who has to dodge too many former lovers is left with nothing but depriving exile:

> *Texas is the place I'd dearly love to be*
> *But all my exes live in Texas*
> *Therefore I reside in Tennessee*

"All My Ex's Live in Texas"
Lyndia J. Shafer and Sanger D. Shafer
for George Strait, 1987

Of course, Texans have no doubt that everyone wants to participate in this paradise. Or do they?

> *By God we're so darn proud to be from Texas - yahoo!*
> *Even of our pride we're proud and we're proud*
>   *of that pride, too*
> *Our pride about our home state is the proudest*
>   *pride indeed*
>
> *And we're proud to be Americans, until we can secede*
> *One more stupid song about Texas*
> *Biggest belt buckles and boasts,*
>   *love that big old Texas toast*
> *Let's sing another stupid Texas song!*

"Stupid Texas Song"
Austin Lounge Lizards, 1998

LOS ANGELES

During the first half of the 20th century blues musicians from the Mississippi Delta migrated almost exclusively to Chicago. In contrast, their Texan colleagues often preferred to move to Los Angeles. That was also the destination for quite a few country music protagonists who had learned their trade in Texas. It is also well known that almost every professional musician in the US lands in LA at some point.

Los Angeles is not really a city, but rather a catastrophe. A terrible, yet wonderful catastrophe, a Moloch that goes against all European ideas of how a city should be planned and function. The city of Los Angeles, in a narrow sense, is home to four million people, but the greater area is much bigger with about eighteen million, and there is no such thing as LA in a narrower sense.

From above, LA looks like leprosy that creeps out over the San Fernando Valley and the otherwise lovely Southern California hills. However, when you get closer, the generous layout and the beauty of the houses, or at least some of the art deco, streamlined *moderne* or Concept houses, turn out to be rather enchanting.

Apparently, one can only either hate or love this monstrosity, and the latter only became clear to me recently. A friend and colleague sang the praises of the city for hours, going on about just how amazingly wonderful it is, all while we were sitting in one of the endless daily LA traffic jams in oppressively hot temperatures and dismal air quality. People who love LA block all that out and don't even see it. Those who hate LA are, of course, found in other parts of the country and particularly in New York City.

For decades, Los Angeles has attracted thousands and thousands of poor laborers from Latin America. However, many others immigrated there because the city is also the heart of the entertainment industry of the western world. It has been a magnet for talent, gifted or not, who have hoped for a great career in the movie, music, TV or porn industry. Naturally, however, not everybody becomes a star, and without a doubt more hopes have been shattered than came true.

Since World War II, Los Angeles has been both the most important film metropolis of the western world and its most relevant center for pop music. However, LA took a long time to develop into the musical hub it is today. In fact, that happened as a side effect of the movie business.

In the 1930s and '40s, Los Angeles already had a vibrant African American music scene. Charles Mingus, the great jazz bassist, was part of it. However, it was short-lived and dissolved as early as the 1950s. But at the same time, the big movie studios began to control and acquire the music industry. In 1956, the Capitol Records Building was opened on Vine Street. The edifice was inspired by a pile of records, replete with a record needle on the roof. Eventually, each of the Hollywood majors would have their own record company, music publishing house and recording studio. Sunset Strip in West Hollywood became the hot spot of live music in the 1960s. Countless bands started from there. The Whisky a Go Go and the Roxy, just a few steps apart, were the springboard for hundreds of artists.

In 1965, The Doors, Linda Ronstadt and Frank Zappa lived a stone's throw apart. Laurel Canyon was home to Canned Heat, Joni Mitchell, Jackson Browne, Crosby, Stills & Nash, as well as John Mayall for a time. Los Angeles is too big and too diverse to have given rise to one common scene or even a sense of community like in San Francisco, Nashville or Atlanta. Los Angeles is heterogeneous and fragmented culturally and artistically. There is always a lot going on there, too many things at the same time, and stylistically there have been a great number of totally different movements. LA is a city of career climbers. Exchange happens elsewhere.

It does not make sense to list individual bands and musicians in the case of Los Angeles, because there are simply too many. On top of that, almost all professional musicians in the USA have moved at some point to Los Angeles or lived close by. Like the film industry, the music industry in Los Angeles attracts talent from the entire world. And even if they were not born there or grew up there, they have to be counted as part of the city's music history.

For local musicians the constant influx of the best and most original artists naturally leads to frustration, feelings of inferiority and increased competition. At first, it was Texas bluesmen like Charles Brown, T-Bone Walker and Lightnin' Hopkins who would come to town, but later came the entire generation of rock and pop artists from Sam Cooke, Bill Withers, Barry White, Bobby Womack, Ike & Tina Turner, John Lennon, David Bowie, to Neil Young,

Melissa Etheridge, Sheryl Crow, Tori Amos, Fleetwood Mac, Jefferson Airplane, The Grateful Dead, Steely Dan, Frank Zappa, Iggy Pop, Motörhead, and so on and so forth....

Beck, Ry Cooder, Etta James, Randy Newman and others were born in LA and The Beach Boys, Captain Beefheart, Cher, Creedence Clearwater Revival and Tom Waits did not have so far to go. They all hailed from a nearby place somewhere in California. But obviously the massive concentration of talent in town proved to be fertile soil for the foundation of bands. Groups like Buffalo Springfield, The Byrds, Canned Heat, The Doors, The Eagles, Guns 'n' Roses, Little Feat, Los Lobos, The Mamas and the Papas, Metallica, Mötley Crue, Rage Against the Machine, Red Hot Chili Peppers and Steppenwolf were all founded in Los Angeles and called it their home.

The producer and inventor of the "Wall of Sound", Phil Spector, was a musical mastermind in Los Angeles like Brian Wilson, the head of the Beach Boys. Both were also similar in their geniality and in their eccentric behavior. Los Angeles has always been a place of longing, especially for those in colder climes:

> *All the leaves are brown*
> *And the sky is grey*
>
> *I'd be safe and warm*
> *If I was in L.A.*
> *California dreamin'*
> *On such a winter's day*

"California Dreamin'"
John and Michelle Phillips, 1966

Homesickness for Los Angeles is largely characterized by a longing for balmy weather and sunshine, but also for drugs, beaches, motorcycle riding and girlfriends:

> *I can almost hear the warm sun shinin' on me*
> *Sniffin' cocaine way down on Malibu Beach*
> *Cruisin' in the canyon with my little woman*
> *Doin' all the talk that I wanna be doin' but*
> *I fall in love again today, I'm a long way from L.A.*

"Long Way from L.A."
Canned Heat, 1971

Some want to go there more than anything, and toy with the idea of dropping everything and going to LA:

> *If I didn't tell her*
> *I could leave today*

"California Dreamin'"
John and Michelle Phillips, 1966

And others really do go to the Promised Land:

> *I left my home in Norfolk Virginia*
> *California on my mind*

"Promised Land"
Chuck Berry, 1964

Or they come for an easy weekend trip, ignore the smog, and decide to stay forever:

> *Took a trip down to LA for a weekend*
> *Let my hair flow and my inspiration grow*

> *On my way to LA*
> *Touch down through the smog cloud, LA runway*
> *In the meantime, on the fault line, California*
>
> *Get a notion, by the ocean, what an idea*
> *Move on over little lover, gonna stay here*

"On My Way to LA"
Phil Carmen, 1985

Arrivals in Los Angeles vary widely. And if you're already high in the plane and trafficking kilos of narcotics, it is pretty euphoric:

> *Coming in from London from over the pole*
> *Flyin' in a big airliner*
> *Chickens flyin' everywhere around the plane*
> *Could we ever feel much finer?*
>
> *Comin' into Los Angeles*
> *Bringin' in a couple of Ks*
> *Don't touch my bags if you please, mister customs man!*

"Coming Into Los Angeles"
Arlo Guthrie, 1969

And as soon as one lands, things get going. However, the euphoria of arriving, the expectation of drugs, sex, warm weather and mobility, turns darker:

> *Drivin' down your freeways*
> *Midnite alleys roam*
> *Cops in cars, the topless bars*
> *Never saw a woman...*
> *So alone, so alone*
> *Motel money murder madness*

> *Let's change the mood*
> *from glad to sadness!*

"L.A. Woman"
Jim Morrison, 1971

Aimless joy rides may be fun, but as soon as one wants to actually arrive somewhere, pretty depressing conditions appear in the form of the fog of drugs and smog and the sheer scale of the city and its nonstop traffic jams:

> *There's a fog upon LA*
> *And my friends have lost their way*
> *We'll be over soon, they said*
> *Now they've lost themselves instead*

"Blue Jay Way"
George Harrison, 1969

Losing yourself is as much of a danger as getting lost in this inhumane city. And despite all the romanticizing of beaches, surfing and parties, the freeway and boulevard are where most Angelinos spend most of their time. One succumbs to loneliness in Los Angeles faster and easier than in other metropolises, in part because the obligation to be in a good mood and the dog-eat-dog world of the entertainment industry don't exactly lend themselves to cozy relationships or reliable friendships. Even being yourself is not that easy when everything blurs. Loneliness and treason go hand in hand. But if your friends let you down, there is always the drugs you can access so effortlessly. In the 1980s and '90s, the deserted center of the city, downtown, had turned into a dangerous drug paradise:

> *I drive on her streets, 'cause she's my companion*
> *I never worry. Now, that is a lie*
>
> *It's hard to believe that there's nobody out there*
> *It's hard to believe that I'm all alone*
> *At least I have her love. The city, she loves me*
> *Lonely as I am. Together we cry*
> *Under the bridge downtown is where I drew some blood*
>
> "Under the Bridge"
Red Hot Chili Peppers, 1991

Los Angeles is an assemblage of small cities across a huge area. One reason for this is the constant risk of earthquakes that prevented high rise construction. As a result, the city consumes the surrounding canyons and hills. People say they live in Culver City, Downtown, West Hollywood, Santa Monica or the Valley. Los Angeles is structured by the transportation arteries that run between them, and they are very sclerotic. It's hard to get the lay of the land in Los Angeles without taking a very close look. The historical center is just now coming into focus for wealthy residents due to its recent renovations. One can spend her life in shabby, depressing parts of town like Burbank or East LA and never even see the ocean or posh and wealthy neighborhoods like Beverly Hills. This is not only due to the enormous social differences but also to the sheer size of the city.

> *The other afternoon*
> *My wife and I*
> *Took a little ride into*
> *Beverly Hills*
> *Went to the private school*
> *Our oldest child attends*

Many famous people send their children there

> "My Life Is Good"
> Randy Newman, 1983

It is unlikely that residents of Bel Air, Beverly Hills, Malibu or Venice Beach often venture to East LA. This is not only due to the vastly different levels of income, to violence, crime or racism. It is also because of the city's transportation grid and its sheer size, which is chaotic and grew somewhat organically but uncontrolled. That means stop and go car traffic for the affluent majority of Angelinos and buses for the rest. The subway that now goes all the way to Santa Monica, has no relevance in daily life. Films like Mika Kaurismäki's *L.A. Without a Map* or Damien Chazelle's *La La Land* illustrate the consequences in a precise and biting caricature.

In Greater Los Angeles it is the highways that the traffic crawls along under the scorching sun, whereas in LA proper they inch between stoplights along boulevards. The latter are not only the city's arteries, but they also lend a hint of character to the respective neighborhoods, almost giving them a face. It is as if Brooklyn and Manhattan were there to justify the Brooklyn Bridge.

> *Century Boulevard (we love it)*
> *Victory Boulevard (we love it)*
> *Santa Monica Boulevard (we love it)*
> *Sixth Street (we love it, we love it)*
> *We love L.A.*

As in every Randy Newman song, it is worth taking a closer look. His sophisticated irony unfolds when you listen closely:

> *Rollin' down the Imperial Highway*
> *With a big nasty redhead at my side*
> *Santa Ana winds blowing hot from the North*
> *And we was born to ride*
>
> *From the South Bay to the Valley*
> *From the West Side to the East Side*
> *Everybody's very happy*
> *'Cause the sun is shining all the time*
> *Looks like another perfect day*
> *I love L.A.*

"I Love L.A."
Randy Newman, 1983

Is he really happy, the narrator of this praise of LA's highways? Well, he must be. After all, everybody is "very happy," and it is "another perfect day" in LA. Any more questions?

The main artery between Downtown and the beach is Santa Monica Boulevard. It runs all the way across Los Angeles County, the most important East-West route. Its character changes along the way. It is a hectic, densely populated commercial street. In Beverly Hills it is urban, in Santa Monica it is a highway. It also leads through wealthy residential neighborhoods like West Los Angeles, Century City and Beverly Hills, but also through metropolitan West Hollywood. Along the road there are car dealerships. It is home to gay and transgender sex workers. However, for many years Los Angeles was considered prudish and homophobic. Gay people were instead drawn to San Francisco or New York City.

> *Yeah, mama and papa told me*
> *I was crazy to stay*
> *I was gay in New York*
> *Just a fag in LA*

"When the Whip Comes Down"
Jagger/Richards, 1978

But that has long since changed. One stretch of Santa Monica Boulevard is West Hollywood Memorial Walk, between Fairfax Avenue and Doheny Drive, a tribute to the victims of AIDS. It is modelled after the famous Hollywood Walk of Fame with its brass stars honoring movie stars embedded in concrete on Hollywood Boulevard. Most people, however, think of Santa Monica Boulevard as the way to go to the beach, a little North of Santa Monica pier with its hotdogs and Ferris wheel. However, the real purpose of this street is to provide you with sufficient time for meditation while you are stuck in traffic. It also provides a particularly somber Angelino pleasure:

> *"All I wanna do is have a little fun before I die"*
> *Says the man next to me out of nowhere [...]*
> *All I wanna do is have some fun*
> *I got a feelin' I'm not the only one*
> *All I wanna do is have some fun*
> *Until the sun comes up over Santa Monica Boulevard*

"All I Wanna Do"
Wyn Cooper, Sheryl Crow,
David Baerwald, Bill Bottrell, Kevin Gilbert, 1994

Fun is a peculiar topic. Fun is used to market all kinds of conceivable and inconceivable goods and services to Americans—immediate fun with no delay, no sacrifice and no anticipation. Instant gratification. Americans don't save money, they run up credit card debt. Any appeal to adulting is met with the accusation of arrogant elitism, and thus stifled. It is all about fun, not about refined enjoyment. We want to, and we have to amuse ourselves to death, as Neil Postman put it, because that is what keeps the economy alive, and it is exactly what the constitution means with "the pursuit of happiness."

> *Livin' down in L.A.*
> *Such a beautiful day*
>
> *People in motion*
> *Our wheels movin' all kind a ways*
>
> *Indoors, outdoors, in the sun*
> *There are people everywhere havin' fun, fun, fun*

"It's a Beautiful Day"
Mike Love and Al Jardine, 1979

Fun is a civic obligation and applied patriotism. And on the West Coast, and particularly in Los Angeles, fun is even a bit more obligatory, banal, flat and tougher. For European taste it is also a bit dark, as if a thread of sense, of impending doom, is woven through it. But Los Angeles is not the city of deep Freudian boring. It is a surface level city with spacious buildings, wide freeways, sparkling street scenes and the film industry. Anyone who denies this, is a lousy party-pooper. Fun in most songs about Los Angeles simply means sex and betrayal:

> *She's a good girl, loves her mama*
> *Loves horses and her boyfriend, too*

> *It's a long day, livin' in Reseda*
> *There's a freeway runnin' through the yard*
> *And I'm a bad boy, 'cause I don't even miss her*
> *I'm a bad boy for breakin' her heart*

"Free Fallin'"
Tom Petty, Jeff Lynne, 1989

At the end of the song, the "bad boy" thinks of his "good girl" as he is "free fallin'" from Mulholland Drive into nothingness. It is remarkable how similar this fantasy of a suicidal leap from Mulholland Drive into the dream factory of Hollywood sounds in a song by R.E.M.:

> *Hollywood is under me*
> *If you ever want to fly*
> *Mulholland Drive*
> *Up in the sky*
> *Stand on a cliff and look down there*
> *Don't be scared, you are alive!*

"Electrolite"
R.E.M., 1996

Fun in Los Angeles is: sex and drugs and rock'n'roll + beaches + the American Dream:

> *Scott gets his hair just perfect*
> *And turns into the light*
>
> *He goes out hunting leopard*
> *In the California night*
> *The big man gets his driver*
> *To bring the car around*
> *He started out with nothing*

> *Just the scuffle nine to five*
> *Now he works the dream machine*
> *Down on Rodeo Drive*

"Rodeo Drive"
Paul Roberts, 1980

The big man who works the soft machine is a functionary of the apparatus, and the apparatus is the dream factory Hollywood or maybe the music industry. From close up, the big man turns out to be a petty worm, a tiny wheel in the big machinery, somebody who has to make a permanent effort to make his life and existence seem bearable:

> *Well, I promo groups when they come into town*
> *Well, they laugh at my toupee,*
>   *they're sure to put me down*
>
> *I got a Corvette and a seersucker suit*
> *Yes, I have*
> *Here comes the bus, uh oh*
> *I thought I had a dime*

"Under Assistant West Coast Promotion Man"
Mick Jagger/Nanker Phelge/Keith Richards, 1965

Not everybody can be a big shot and have their name on a star on Hollywood Boulevard. Many, in fact most, struggle in vain for glory and immortal fame.

> *You can see all the stars as you walk*
>   *down Hollywood Boulevard*
> *People who worked and suffered and struggled for fame*
> *Some who succeeded and some who suffered in vain*

> *Everybody's a dreamer and everybody's a star*
> *And everybody's in show biz,*
> *   it doesn't matter who you are*
> *Success walks hand in hand with failure*
> *Along Hollywood Boulevard*

"Celluloid Heroes"
Ray Davies, 1972

The pull of the entertainment industry is irresistible. Hundreds of hopeful potential studio audience members linger in front of the sound stages whenever live shows are taping. They hope for a second of fame and TO BE ON TV when the camera pans the room. The enormous film, TV, music, gameshow and porn industries constantly need vast amounts of raw meat. As fodder, the young talents fight for attention and a spot in the Hollywood limelight. Parents invest in their children to take a bus to Hollywood so they can be discovered.

> *She drew out all her money out of the Southern Trust*
> *And put her little boy aboard a Greyhound bus*
> *Leaving Louisiana for the Golden West*
> *Down came the tears from her happiness*
> *Her own little son named Johnny B. Goode*
> *Was gonna make some motion pictures out in Hollywood*

"Bye Bye Johnny"
Chuck Berry, 1960

And once you have made it, you are not going to be a better human being. But you may see more clearly behind the curtain as to what the Hollywood apparatus is really like.

> *You spin like the Cadillac was*
> *Overturning down a cliff on television*
> *And the radio is on, and the radioman is speaking*
> *And the radioman says women were a curse*
> *So, men built Paramount Studios*
> *And men built Columbia Studios*
> *And men built Los Angeles [...]*
>
> *Gone savage for teenagers with*
> *Automatic weapons and boundless love*
> *Gone savage for teenagers who are*
> *Aesthetically pleasing*
> *In other words: Fly!*
> *Los Angeles beckons the teenagers*
> *To come to her on buses*
> *Los Angeles loves love*
>
> "Screenwriter's Blues"
> Soul Coughing, 1994

And if you don't make it, you may start to hate the shiny, happy people of Beverly Hills or Laurel Canyon.

> *Well, I hear that Laurel Canyon*
> *Is full of famous stars*
> *But I hate them worse than lepers*
> *And I'll kill them in their cars...*
>
> "Revolution Blues"
> Neil Young, 1974

It is pretty obvious that the particularly superficial kind of Los Angeles fun, which has much to do with illusions but also with sex and drugs and wealth, looks very sad under the sunny skies of Southern California. That is not just a mere fiction of snobbish Europeans who blithely snub

American materialism. Those who pull the levers in the dream machine, mostly white men, are neither stupid nor insensitive and they have finely tuned antennae for this reality. Los Angeles has the blues. The counterculture recognizes this, but the commercial mainstream entertainment industry denies and suppresses it. It does everything it can to conjure up the opposite feeling. Problems? Blues? We don't have those here. There is nothing but blue skies above, and everybody: be fucking happy all the time. After all, Los Angeles has it all. It is your own fault if you don't like it here.

> *If you got sunshine and beaches,*
> *how can that be so hard?*
> *And maybe oranges and grapefruit*
> *in your own backyard*
>
> *If you have mountains and the ocean*
> *and a great, big smiling sky*
> *There's very little that is blue here.*
> *So, the blues passed Los Angeles by*

"Los Angeles Blues"
Peggy Lee and Quincy Jones, 1961

In the land of the free, the pursuit of happiness is not just a constitutional right, rather it is a civic duty. And there is no place more competent and experienced in the production, but also in the consumption, of happiness than Los Angeles, where no one can be too sad. That's against the law, especially where fame itself is at home, in the Hollywood Hills:

> *He'd headed West 'cause he felt that a change*
> *Would do him good*

> *She had been born with a face that would*
>   *let her get her way*
> *He saw that face and he lost all control*
>
> *And those Hollywood nights*
> *In those Hollywood hills*
> *All those big city nights*
> *In those high rolling hills*

"Hollywood Nights"
Bob Seger, 1978

It is no surprise that the Midwestern boy will leave the Hollywood Hills again after this bitter disappointment. Another song by another band bids his farewell:

> *Now, this is not the time or the place*
> *For a broken-hearted*
> *'Cause this is the end of the rainbow*
> *Where no one can be too sad*
>
> *Bye-bye, Hollywood Hills!*
> *I'm gonna come back to walk these streets again*

"Hollywood Hills"
Samu Haber for Sunrise Avenue, 2011

The sad farewell to Hollywood is as common as the euphoria upon arriving. After all, almost everyone fails. The trick is to fail elegantly. Crushed dreams are the rule. Happy is he who gains inner strength and philosophical wisdom from the experience:

> *Bobby's driving through the city tonight*
> *It's a scene down on Sunset Boulevard*

> *So many faces in and out of my life*
> *Life is a series of hellos and good-byes*
> *I'm afraid it's time for good-bye again*
>
> *Say goodbye to Hollywood*
> *Say goodbye, my baby!*

"Say Goodbye to Hollywood"
Billy Joel, 1976

In many ways Los Angeles is the end of the rainbow. And indeed, it is where the Western World ends.

> *It's the edge of the world and all of Western civilization*
> *The sun may rise in the East. At least it's settled*
>   *in a final location*
> *It's understood that Hollywood sells Californication*

"Californication"
Red Hot Chili Peppers, 1999

The American ideology of Manifest Destiny bumps up against its geographical limits here at the edge of the world and all of Western civilization. "Go West, young man," loses its meaning when you are looking out at the Pacific Ocean. Bands with ties to Los Angeles, like The Doors or Creedence Clearwater Revival, made no secret of their end-time fantasies.

> *Well, I woke up this morning, and I got myself a beer*
> *The future's uncertain, and the end is always near*

"Roadhouse Blues"
The Doors, 1970

> *I hear hurricanes a-blowing*
> *I know the end is coming soon*

"Bad Moon Rising"
John Fogerty, 1969

> *Ride the highway west, baby! [...]*
> *This is the end, beautiful friend*
> *This is the end, my only friend, the end*

"The End"
The Doors, 1966

Poverty, drugs, the smog, dashed dreams, the high crime rate and a permanent traffic jam: of course, these living conditions are not exactly in line with the dreams and promises produced in the City of Angels. Los Angeles has always chewed up everyone and spit them out. The grindstone of forced fun, superficiality, and extreme competition turn everything into dust. They get to everybody, even the winners. Most of all, however, it seems clear from the point of view of those who once came to Los Angeles full of hopes and have now seen all their dreams shattered that the city is going to slide into the ocean at some point.

> *Oh it's so good to know*
> *That it's all just a show for you*
> *But when the suppers are planned*
> *And the freeways are crammed*
> *And the mountains erupt*
> *And the Valley is sucked*
> *Into cracks in the earth*

"L.A."
Neil Young, 1973

The scientists, mystics, and statistics foretell the downfall of Los Angeles. And when the city is finally swallowed up by the Pacific it will be due to its own sinful existence. Openly or secretly, Americans, Puritan or not, yearn for a millenarian apocalyptic end:

> *This old town is filled with sin*
> *It'll swallow you in*
>
> *This old earthquake's gonna leave me in the poor house*
> *It seems like this whole town's insane*
>
> *The scientists say*
> *It will all wash away*

"Sin City"
Gram Parsons, 1969

The most disillusioned do not shed a tear over their faded fantasy:

> *And if California slides into the ocean*
> *Like the mystics and statistics say it will*
> *I predict this motel will be standing until I pay my bill*
>
> *I was sitting in the Hollywood Hawaiian Hotel*
> *I was listening to the air conditioner hum*

"Desperados under the Eaves"
Warren Zevon, 1976

Los Angeles is the end of the world as we know it. The end-time mood there is not only due to the failure of so many hopeful talents or the city's position on the extreme margin of the North American continent. One natural catastrophe after another haunts Los Angeles. The best known among them are earthquakes. The city lies on the San Andreas and the Puente Hills fault lines, which have caused nine major quakes since 1800 as well as thousands of smaller ones. In 1971, about sixty people died in the Sylmar Earthquake, and the Northridge Earthquake in 1994 killed fifty-seven. Almost every day smaller tremblors are recorded. But everyone is waiting for the Big One that will finally raze the city for good. It seems like the justified fear of the Big One is conflated with an almost apocalyptic expectation and euphoric longing for biblical punishment for the immoral life in Sodom and Gomorrah.

The dry climate and the depletion of water reserves by Angelinos cause wildfires to rage around the city. On a warm November morning in 1961, fire erupted north of Bel Air, a rich area of Los Angeles, and was fanned by the hot Santa Ana winds. In two days it turned five hundred homes into ashes, mostly owned by wealthy Angelinos, many Hollywood stars amongst them. Because the fire mostly affected the rich and famous of the city, it was soon called a "tragedy trimmed in mink." Lightnin' Hopkins said it like this:

> *Oh they had a big fire down in L.A.*
>   *(well in Beverly Hills or somewhere a little close).*
>   *All them buildings is burnin' down*
> *Well you know they didn't have enough water*
>   *to put out the fire.*
>   *250-some home they got burnin' down*

"Burnin' in L.A."
Lightnin' Hopkins, 1962

But floods and mudslides are also no strangers to LA.

They are closely related to the forest fires. In 1933, a wild fire destroyed all of the vegetation above Montrose-La Crescenta. When it rained on New Year's Eve 1934, the entire region flooded. About fifty people perished in the high waters. Woody Guthrie's song speaks of one hundred:

> *One hundred souls were taken*
> *In that fatal New Year's Flood*
>
> *Our highways were blockaded*
> *Our bridges all washed down*
> *Our houses wrecked and scattered*
> *As the flood came a-rumblin' down*
>
> "Los Angeles New Year's Flood"
> Woody Guthrie, 1938

In 1972, Albert Hammond wanted us to believe that "it never rains in Southern California." The truth, however, is a different story: It pours, man, it pours. But people dig the victims and their cars from the mud again and again. And they start anew. These catastrophes are typical of LA and are manmade. Excessive water use has turned the land around Los Angeles into a desert and a lot of it has been paved over by asphalt and concrete. The creeks and rivers have been channelized. It is overpopulated and because real estate is expensive, houses and mansions have been built even in the most inhospitable locations.

This too has been commented on by Lightnin' Hopkins in his music. In 1969, he sang about a double catastrophe that struck Los Angeles in January and February of that year. On January 18, 1969, heavy rain began to fall. It lasted ten days. Eighty-seven people died in the subsequent floods and landslides, not counting dozens of victims of car accidents.

And this time it did not hit the rich. On the contrary. Even as repairs were being carried out on hundreds of destroyed buildings and bridges, another downpour began that lasted ten days and killed another twenty-one people.

> *People all told me, "You know, if you go to*
> * Los Angeles, Lightnin', you makin' a sad mistake"*
> *But I hollered: "*
> *If you stop having them mudslides, I tell you,*
> * I may make that my home and I may stay"*
>
> *I couldn't do nothing but break down and begin to cry*
> *When I heard about Los Angeles under water,*
> * ain't nobody got no time*

"Los Angeles Blues"
Lightnin' Hopkins, 1969

Here, Lightnin' Hopkins shows class, defiance, and solidarity with the victims. That's in contrast to Richard Harris, the singer, and Jimmy Webb, who is to blame for the lyrics of "MacArthur Park".

Douglas MacArthur was a highly decorated general in the Second World War and Korean War. Situated on Wilshire Boulevard in Westlake, Los Angeles, MacArthur Park is a small, lovely park around an artificial lake. "MacArthur Park" is often elected by the music press as the song with the worst lyrics of all time. Even Michelle Shocked made fun of the sweet green icing of "MacArthur Park". In "Come a Long Way", the protagonist kicks in the repo man's door, grabs her 920 motorbike and goes on a long trip through various neighborhoods of Los Angeles, going 500 miles in just one day. It is a love song to LA. And perhaps even to MacArthur Park.

> *I heard the screams of the dying dark*
> *Through the sweet green icing of MacArthur Park*

"Come a Long Way"
Michelle Shocked, 1992

But here is the lyrical high point of MacArthur Park itself and, on this high note, this chapter on the metropolis of the West Coast should find its heavily symbolic and saccharine finale:

> *MacArthur Park is melting in the dark*
> *All the sweet, green icing flowing down*
> *Someone left a cake out in the rain*
> *I don't think that I can take it*
> *'Cause it took so long to bake it*
> *And I'll never have that recipe again*
> *Oh no!*
> *Oh no*
> *No*
> *Oh no!*

"MacArthur Park"
Jimmy Webb for Richard Harris, 1968

SAN FRANCISCO

San Francisco is different. And really different from Los Angeles. Of course, it is in California, but it feels a little bit like London or maybe even Edinburgh. That's because of the weather. San Francisco is a fog magnet, the perfect place for people who like drizzle and want to wear coats in the middle of summer. It is almost always cold and foggy in the morning before the California sun burns off the marine layer.

There is not a lot of remarkable music from San Francisco, but there are a few beautiful songs about the city. Our history of music from San Francisco may be short, but it needs to be told. Not much innovation happened there. The creative impulses usually came from somewhere else. The Grateful Dead are a remarkable exception. However, San Francisco is the city most strongly associated with the social and cultural revolution of the 1960s. We may chuckle about the movement today, but we continue to benefit from it. And of course, it echoes in the music. As a result, songs about San Francisco need to be divided into those before and after 1967. That's because the 1967 "Summer of Love" first blossomed in San Francisco. Naturally, there are also commercial love songs in which picturesque San Francisco is merely a thankful, yet rather coincidental backdrop.

Before the Summer of Love, it is no surprise songs were about the city's unique microclimate. It is clear that the then 24-year-old Bob Dylan was apparently not yet truly familiar with the Bay Area's meteorological quirks when he wrote and sang these lines:

> *San Francisco is fine, you sure get lots of sun*
> *But I'm used to four seasons, California's got but one*

> "California"
> Bob Dylan, 1965

In reality, however, it does rain in San Francisco whenever the city is not shrouded in fog. At least subjectively. The weather charts don't show all that much annual precipitation. And very little in summer. But the large number of songs about fog and rain in the city by the bay indicate that I am not alone in my personal impression of grey skies, cold, and rain in San Francisco. And that this rain truly has its own appeal, especially when reminisced from a distance.

> *Why the hell am I here today*
>
> *It ain't bad, but it ain't San Francisco in the rain*
> *A guitar mourning through the crashing ocean waves*

> "San Francisco Rain"
> Grahame Lesh, 2012

The similarly worldly and seasoned Tony Bennett knew what was up. He knew the sun over San Francisco, but also the cold morning marine layer:

I left my heart in San Francisco

The morning fog may chill the air

Above the blue and windy sea
When I come home to you, San Francisco
Your golden sun will shine for me

"I Left My Heart in San Francisco"
George Cory and Douglass Cross
for Tony Bennett, 1953

"I Left My Heart in San Francisco" may be Tony Bennett's trademark song, but many others have sung beautiful versions of it that have become standards, including Frank Sinatra (1957), July London (1963) and, last but not least, Van Morrison (2017).

The noteworthy weather in San Francisco and its tourist attractions, like the cable cars, are thematized in insignificant, sappy hits about the city. But a few songs also take on the darker sides of the city or make it a setting for heartache. One of the more idiosyncratic ones is "Come Back from San Francisco":

Come back from San Francisco!
It can't be all that pretty

Should pretty boys in discos distract you from your novel
Remember I'm awful in love with you!

"Come Back from San Francisco"
Stephin Merritt
for The Magnetic Fields, 1999

Musically, this song is pleasantly minimalistic and its

lyrics are tinged with irony, as the singer claims: "You need me like the wind needs the trees to blow in, like the moon needs poetry, you need me." Of course, the wind needs trees and the moon poems—urgently! But it is not really San Francisco the lovesick singer is serenading. That is more the case in Jesse Fuller's absolutely beautiful "San Francisco Bay Blues" where he depicts San Francisco Bay as the locus of his suffering. His beloved has left him and he is destroyed and filled with self-reproach and longing. This time, however, it is the spurned lover who is left behind in San Francisco:

> *I got the blues from my baby,*
>   *left me by the San Francisco Bay*
> *She take the ocean liner,*
>   *and she's gone so far away*
>
> *She said goodbye, she like to make me cry,*
>   *I want to lay down and die*
>
> *If I ever get her back to stay,*
>   *it's gonna be another brand new day*
> *Walking with my baby down by*
>   *the San Francisco Bay*

"San Francisco Bay Blues"
Jesse Fuller, 1954

Of all the great renditions of this song, I find the one by Jesse Fuller himself—both the studio version and his live recording from the Newport Jazz Festival—most convincing. Likewise, Eric Clapton's version on his *Unplugged* album. But there is also a very distinctive version worth listening to by the gifted bassist Colin Hodgkinson in which he sings accompanied only by his own bass.

But San Francisco Bay became famous in pop music due to a different song. "The Dock of the Bay" tells the tale of a stranded man, similar to the protagonist in "Detroit City (I Wanna Go Home)" by Bobby Bare in 1963, who has travelled a long way as a migrant worker and now that he's reached his destination is overcome by a peculiar melancholy and lethargy in this foreign place.

> *I left my home in Georgia*
> *And I headed for the Frisco Bay*
>
> *I'm just come sittin' on the dock of the bay*
>
> *I'm sittin' here restin' my bones*
> *And this loneliness won't leave me alone*
> *Two thousand miles I roamed*
> *Just to make this dock my home*
>
> "(Sittin' on) The Dock of the Bay"
> Redding/Cropper, 1967

If you leave the city and drive north on US 101 over the Golden Gate Bridge, you can see the iconic prison island, Alcatraz, on the right. And soon after you reach the headlands of breathtakingly beautiful Marin County, things get worse. An offramp leads to San Quentin. It is not only the oldest prison in California but is known as one of the most brutal and overcrowded. To date, approximately 500 inmates have been executed there by hanging, gas, or lethal injection. Apparently, conditions are terrible. In 1967, felons founded the militant neo-Nazi group Aryan Brotherhood at San Quentin, also nicknamed "The Arena".

San Quentin became famous in the music world due to one

of the best live albums in the history of popular music: Johnny Cash's, *At San Quentin* (1969). That was the first time Cash publicly performed the song, "San Quentin", which he had written especially for that evening:

> *San Quentin, you've been livin' hell to me*
> *San Quentin, I hate every inch of you*
> *San Quentin, what good do you think you do?*
> *Do you think I'll be different when you're through?*
> *San Quentin, may you rot and burn in hell!*
> *And may all the world regret you did no good!*

"San Quentin"
Johnny Cash, 1969

One can still hear how emotional the inmates became, thanks to the live recording. Cash also enjoyed it. He played the song twice that night and both versions are documented on the live album.

This was the fourth time Cash had played for the prisoners in San Quentin. At an earlier concert in 1958, a certain Merle Haggard was so impressed by Cash that he launched his own impressive career as a country singer once he got out. Haggard spent three years at San Quentin for jail break while serving time for a robbery conviction.

San Quentin may have been a "livin' hell," but most people long to see San Francisco. And when they arrive, they are glad to finally get a chance to meet the city. Yet the following song is about an unfaithful lover. Apparently, the like is very frequently drawn to San Francisco.

> *Hello, hello San Francisco!*
> *Woh, we finally got a chance to meet*

> *You know I love, I love Chicago*
> *But some of my good friends told me that my baby*
> *   was headed toward that Golden Gate*
>
> *You know, I heard she had a boyfriend,*
> *   and this cat's name was Buddy Joe*
> *And he was running a game down on Philco*
>
> *Oh somebody, somebody better tell me,*
> *   where in the world can this Philco Street be found*
> *You know, I'm gonna find my woman down there.*

"Hello San Francisco"
Robert Geddins for Buddy Guy, 1972

Buddy Guy does sing about a "Philco Street." However, he probably meant Fillmore Street which in his pronunciation would indeed sound something like "Philmoh." Fillmore Street runs through the Western Addition, which was a thriving Black post-WWII neighborhood. The same Fillmore Street is referenced in Lowell Fulson's simple and straightforward, "San Francisco Blues":

> *Suitcase packed, trunk's already gone.*
> *   Going to San Francisco to make it my home, yeah*
> *San Francisco, please make room for me!*
>
> *Take me to Fillmore Street!*
> *   It's the place to be.*
>
> *Well, I'm going to San Francisco,*
> *   if I have to crawl on my knees*

"San Francisco Blues"
Lowell Fulson, 1948

Like in songs about Los Angeles and Memphis, the arrival in the city is a frequent topic in songs about San Francisco. Arrivals are something special, ceremonial. In comparison, One of the most well-known pop songs of all time is also about an arrival to San Francisco like the one Lowell Fulson describes. And now with this song, we get to what San Francisco has meant for the last half century. The year is 1967, and the Western World is about to change dramatically. The origin of this cultural revolution is San Francisco and the Monterey International Pop Music Festival in June of 1967. "San Francisco (Be Sure to Wear Flowers in Your Hair)" is the undisputed anthem of this movement.

If you're going to San Francisco
Be sure to wear some flowers in your hair

For those who come to San Francisco
Summertime will be a love-in there

All across the nation
There's a whole generation
With a new explanation

"San Francisco (Be Sure to Wear Flowers in Your Hair)"
John Phillips for Scott McKenzie, 1967

Just like the Beatles or the Rolling Stones represent the first half of the 1960s, this song, and that which it symbolizes, stand for the latter. It was the children of World War II soldiers on both sides of the Atlantic that called for a better society and more freedom to breathe. Against the backdrop of the war in Vietnam, they questioned patriarchal and authoritarian social structures and called for civil courage over civil obedience. "San Francisco (Be Sure to Wear

Flowers in Your Hair)" captured the countercultural movement and its birth during the Summer of Love. Naive but catchy. The Hippies or Flower Children as well as the smell of pot that came with them quickly became the latest nightmare for the conservative and bigoted society of the time. Even relatively liberal country musicians like the aforementioned Merle Haggard attacked the San Francisco longhairs:

> *We don't smoke marijuana in Muskogee*
> *We don't take our trips on LSD*
> *We don't let our hair grow long and shaggy*
> *Like the hippies out in San Francisco do*
> *I'm proud to be an Okie from Muskogee*

"Okie from Muskogee"
Merle Haggard, 1969

Just a decade earlier, the enemies of bourgeoise society and the danger to youth had been the rock 'n' rollers, and particularly the pelvis-pumping and lascivious-eyed Elvis Presley. His appropriation of Black music was interpreted as "passing as Black" and as an attack on the foundations of the Baby Boomer society, segregation. But this new thing here was even more dangerous: these were intellectuals who had found their own pop cultural form of expression and put the whole capitalistic societal order in question, as well as any other form of imperialism, particularly the war in Vietnam. The epicenter of this seismic event was the Haight-Ashbury neighborhood of San Francisco, where artists, activists, dropouts and musicians gathered for all kinds of love-ins, demonstrations, sessions, and psychedelic drug experiments. The establishment was alarmed, and the cops beat up the flower children whenever they could. Eric Burdon poignantly described the feeling in San Francisco during the Summer of Love:

This following program is dedicated to the city and people of San Francisco, who may not know it but they are beautiful, and so is their city.

> *Strobe lights beam creates dreams*
> *Walls move, minds do, too*
>
> *Old child, young child, feel alright*
> *On a warm San Franciscan night*
>
> *I wasn't born there. Perhaps I'll die there*
> *There's no place left to go, San Francisco!*

"San Franciscan Nights"
The Animals, 1967

The "Summer of Love" didn't endure, though it lasted two summers, so to speak. The festival in Monterey in 1967, was followed by the enormous undertaking in Woodstock, New York, in August of 1969 and an orgy of violence at the Altamont Speedway in northern California the following December. By then "peace, love and understanding" had transformed into mayhem. Murder and racist rocker gangs marked the end of the Haight-Ashbury dream. The movement was discredited. The Rolling Stones, who later were forced to experience the murder of Meredith Hunter at Altamont by the Hells Angels (and reacted with a furious rendition of "Sympathy for the Devil"), always had a strong sense of the times. Long before Altamont, in March of 1969, they recorded "Gimme Shelter" as a response to the horrors of the Vietnam War and the deteriorating situation in the country.

> *Ooh, see the fire is sweepin'*
> *Our very street today*
> *Burns like a red coal carpet [...]*
> *War, children, it's just a shot away*

"Gimme Shelter"
Jagger/Richards, 1969

Altamont was the swan song of the 1960s. In any case, it marks the sober awakening from the idealistic dream of a better world through music, drugs, free love, meditation, expanding consciousness and brotherly love. The concert ended with three deaths and Marty Balin of Jefferson Airplane being knocked out by a Hells Angel.

Violence had come home. From the massacres in Vietnam to the streets of the US. Drug problems exploded, also as a direct result of the war, and the civil rights movement was met with clubs, tear gas and live bullets. Violence spiraled upward, playing out in the shadow of the nuclear threat of the Cold War.

However, a psychedelic band, which was the most important expression of the new mood, next to Jimi Hendrix, survived. In May of 1965, Jerry Garcia, Bob Weir, Ron Pigpen McKernan, Dana Morgan Jr. and Bill Kreutzmann made their first appearance at a Pizzeria in Menlo Park, near San Francisco, under the name Warlocks. They hung out in Haight-Ashbury. As the Grateful Dead around the guitarist Jerry Garcia, they became iconic of the psychedelic, LSD-fueled Flower Power culture. They are also San Francisco's greatest contribution to music history. To this day, countless "Deadheads" from around the world make the pilgrimage to the band's original commune at 710 Ashbury Street to worship at the shrine.

The Dead were always a little bit spacy. From the elevated position of musicians who were totally dedicated to self-discovery and the use of LSD, that is to say from "eight miles high," humanity's problems suddenly seemed manageable. The sense of scale changed with the order of magnitude of your exploding consciousness.

> *Standing on the moon, I see the battle rage below*
> *There's a metal flag beside me*
> *Old Glory standing stiffly, crimson, white and indigo*
>
> *I hear the cries of children and the other songs of war*
> *It's like a mighty melody that rings down from the sky*
> *Standing here upon the moon I watch it all roll by*

"Standing On the Moon"
Robert Hunter/Jerry Garcia, 1989

The Grateful Dead gave countless free concerts, putting half of Haight-Ashbury out of commission, were the first band to allow bootleg recordings for personal use, and made no secret of their drug habit. Jerry Garcia's extended improvisations that often lasted for fifteen minutes became legendary, until they too finally concluded. In 1995, Garcia died at a rehab in Marin County at the young age of 53. That marked the end of the era.

One of the most beautiful songs about San Francisco, but also about more than that, was penned by Robert Hunter and Jerry Garcia. Of course, it is about rain in San Francisco and, more specifically, about rain in the Mission District, one of the city's oldest neighborhoods. The Mission has long been home to a thriving native Spanish-speaking population. But the drug treatment centers on 14th Street attract many homeless, hopeless and neglected people. Despite all the gentrification that has been going on there since the first tech boom in the 1990s, parts of the Mission are very rough, hardly much better than Skid Row in Los Angeles.

> *It was midnight in the Mission*
>   *and the bells were not for me*
> *Walking along in the Mission in the rain*
>
> *Ten years ago I walked this street,*
>   *my dreams were riding tall*
> *Tonight, I would be thankful, Lord,*
>   *for any dreams at all*
>
> *There's some satisfaction in the San Francisco rain*
> *No matter what comes down,*
>   *the Mission always looks the same*

"Mission in the Rain"
Robert Hunter/Jerry Garcia, 1976

MAP OF
ST LOUIS MO

ST. LOUIS

All over St. Louis [...]
All the cats wanna dance with
Sweet Little Sixteen

> "Sweet Little Sixteen"
> Chuck Berry, 1958

Chuck Berry knew what he was singing about in 1958. He was born in 1926 in St. Louis and grew up there. When he was eighteen, he robbed three shops in Kansas City, which resulted in three years of incarceration at a youth detention facility. This is where he started to practice the guitar. In his song "Bio", Berry talks about what happened next:

I was living in St. Louis
In the year of nineteen fifty-five

He then goes on to describe his and his five siblings' modest upbringing. But then he...

Hitch hiked to Chicago
Just to hear Muddy Waters play...

Berry really did take a trip to Chicago with a friend from school in May of 1955 to hear Howlin' Wolf, Elmore James, and Muddy Waters.

> *I asked him what I could do to make it*
> *And it was he who showed me the way*

"Bio"
Chuck Berry, 1973

Muddy Waters sent him to Chess Records and in short order Leonard Chess personally produced Berry's songs "Maybellene" and "Wee Wee Hours" on May 21st, 1955. Berry was accompanied by Willie Dixon, Chess's studio bass player, ongoing co-producer, and maybe the most important blues songwriter of all time.

If there ever was a birthday for rock music, it was on this day in May. Berry took inspiration from the 1938 song "Ida Red" by Bob Wills and his Texas Playboys. But what he came up with in the end was something entirely new.

There was a dominating, distorted electric guitar reminiscent of the Chicago blues and the likes of Muddy Waters, Howlin' Wolf and, most of all, Elmore James. In many instances, Berry virtually copied entire intros by James. However, in Berry's music, the guitar structures the whole song. No longer was it just the element that would echo the singer in the custom of call and response, like in West African music such as griots, which continued on from field hollers to church sermons and even doo wop songs.

Guitar heroes were not the most important inspiration for his very complex playing. Instead, what makes his playing so unique is that he oriented himself along the lines of piano player's persistent triplet style, most noticeably that of Big Joe Turner. He also stole from his own sidekick Johnny

Johnson's keyboard style and imitated it on a semi-acoustic Gibson.

Chuck Berry remains hard to copy to this day because of how he almost always played double stops, simultaneously striking at least two strings at a time with near constant insistence on blue notes (an African inheritance which is not easily depicted on a European scale) which he bent in various ways. Every tone played by Chuck Berry can always be immediately recognized as his, as is only true for very few guitarists like B. B. King, Eric Clapton or Keith Richards.

Berry not only gave birth to rock'n'roll (despite Bill Haley, Elvis Presley, Jerry Lee Lewis, Little Richard and others claiming the title of "King of Rock 'n' Roll"). It can be rightfully claimed that by playing together, Dixon, Johnson and especially Berry, basically created the genre of rock music. Today it is impossible to imagine a rock song that is not built on Berry's guitar playing and his way of storytelling. In 1984, Bruce Springsteen said it plainly:

> *We learned more from a three-minute record, baby*
> *Than we ever learned in school*

"No Surrender"
Bruce Springsteen, 1984

Springsteen is not being ironic. And if you listen to Chuck Berry you know what he means. Berry told stories not just about the generation of pimply baby-boomers. They spoke to a wide audience. They told of the perspective of this first generation who grew up in material comfort without cares and without goals beyond consumerism. The Korean War was short by US standards and long forgotten. Baby-boomers had every imaginable convenience but found no meaning in middle class suburban life in a culture of sexual repression and conformity. This new generation of alienated teenagers lived in two worlds: one was "school days," boring, uneventful and prudish, while the other was the promise of rock 'n' roll with its new youth culture of hot rod racing, flirting, and the "beat loud and bold…"

> *When the teacher was gone,*
>   *that's when we had a ball […]*
> *We had a portable radio, we was ballin' the jacks*
> *But we'd be all back in order when the teacher got back*

"Oh Baby Doll"
Chuck Berry, 1957

You may have danced in the school bathrooms, but you still would only quaff soft drinks. You would wear your hair short and respect your elders. But those were already the "days of old." Deliverance, however, was seen in the vague promises of rock 'n' roll, of a more exciting future at hand:

> *Soon as three o'clock rolls around […]*
> *Close up your books, get out of your seat*
> *Down the halls and into the street […]*
> *Right to the juke joint, you go in […]*
> *Drop the coin right into the slot*
> *You're gotta hear somethin' that's really hot*
>
> *Hail, hail rock and roll*
> *Deliver me from the days of old!*

"School Days"
Chuck Berry, 1957

While Berry's approach to guitar playing was totally new, his other innovation was his ability to capture the times in a story the length of a 45 single. For this, he deserves the Nobel Prize no less than Bob Dylan. Again: "We learned more from a three-minute record than we ever learned in school."

Even while Elvis Presley was having enormous success, bringing Black rhythm and blues culture to a White audience as if it were new or, even, his very own, the real savior was Chuck Berry. But Chuck Berry's record company hid the fact he was Black.

However, Chuck Berry *was* Black. In fact, he was the only well-known African-American rock 'n' roll star besides Little Richard and Fats Domino. (Only Little Richard, the charismatic singer and frenetic piano-player from Macon, Georgia, accepted Chuck Berry as a peer. Berry, he decided, was, "a good, Black Berry. My mother used to make black-berry jam.")

Macon, Georgia, St. Louis, Missouri, the 1950s: days of strict segregation, lynch mobs, and Jim Crow. The life of a nationally known Black musician was like running the gauntlet when playing in the South. Berry was repeatedly thrown in jail and often, as in December 1959 in St. Louis, sentenced by all White juries and racist judges. In that particular instance, his crime was crossing a state line with a 14-year-old girl.

Chuck Berry was St. Louis's shining star. His 1958 autobiographical song "Johnny B. Goode" was sent symbolically into space aboard the Voyager 1 spacecraft because it was found worthy to represent humanity. But in his youth, the same young successful musician, Charles Edward Anderson Berry, was not even allowed to enter the theater in his segregated hometown.

In 1986, Berry triumphantly celebrated his sixtieth birthday in the fabulous 4,500-seat Fox Theatre in downtown St.

Louis. To appear with him, he invited a few close friends who were not exactly unknown: Keith Richards, Eric Clapton, Linda Ronstadt, Julian Lennon, Etta James, Robert Cray and, of course, Johnny Johnson. It was a frank and triumphant statement by an African-American of huge accomplishment: Here I am, formerly marginalized and harassed but now calling the shots up here onstage. It was just as he'd pictured it in 1955:

> *Someday you will be a man*
> *And you will be the leader of a big old band*
> *Many people coming from miles around*
> *To hear you play your music when the sun go down*
> *Maybe someday your name will be in lights...*

"Jonny B. Goode"
Chuck Berry, 1955

Bob Dylan also planned to attend Berry's birthday concert but, due to illness, could not. The director, Taylor Hackford, captured this remarkable show in his documentary *Hail, Hail Rock 'n' Roll*. Anyone interested in Chuck Berry or St. Louis, or both, has got to see this film.

Big Joe Williams also grew up in St. Louis. He was born there in 1903, although he spent his life as a vagrant blues musician. He is said to have played in every state in the union but always returned to his hometown, the so-called Gateway to the West.

In 1965, the city constructed the architecturally spectacular Gateway Arch that rises 630 feet over the Mississippi. This is where the Southern section of the famous Route 66 starts:

> *Well, it goes through St. Louis [...]*
> *Get your kicks on Route 66!*

"Route 66"
Bobby Troup for Nat King Cole, 1946

But Route 66 is long gone.

St. Louis was once also a key railroad hub. That's over, too. People fly these days. Now the airports in Chicago and Atlanta are the biggest in the US, dwarfing St. Louis. One would suspect an important port at the confluence of the Mississippi and Missouri River. And there once was one, but that too is long gone. Today St. Louis is primarily in the headlines for racial unrest, high crime, and murder rates. There are still two freight train depots, and they are both in East St. Louis, on the other side of the river in Illinois. Like many twin cities, St. Louis also has an ugly little sister. Minneapolis has St. Paul, Kansas City, Missouri, has Kansas City, Kansas, and St. Louis has East St. Louis. As described earlier, there was a time when rail lines were the pulsing arteries of the country. The legendary Wabash Cannonball which, incidentally, never really existed, immortalized in song, turned its back on St. Louis and went straight for its little sister in Illinois:

> *And now she goes to Memphis, Mattoon, New Mexico*
> *Flies to East St. Louis, Lord, she never does it slow*

"The Wabash Cannonball"
traditional, End of the 19th C.

Tempi passati. Today East St. Louis is eponymous with misery:

> *And you're east of East St. Louis and the wind*
>   *is making speeches,*
> *And it's true, there's nothing left for him down here*

> "Time"
> Tom Waits, 1985

"East of East St. Louis?" That's often considered another name for "Hell on Earth." East St. Louis has often had one of the highest murder rates in the US. Its heavy industry, based on the rail depots, folded. Most of those who could leave, did. The city continues to shrink. Many of those left behind do not have a good education and have given up hope. The White middle class has gone. Currently 98% of the population is Black. But, also, the Black middle class, such as Miles Davis' family, has vanished.

In 1927, the upper middle-class Davis family moved to East St. Louis with little one-year-old Miles. Miles was born north of St. Louis in the same year as Chuck Berry. His father was a dentist and even owned real estate. At the time, East St. Louis was a preferred Black middle-class suburb, only ten years after one of the worst pogroms in the history of the USA when, in 1917, a White mob killed fifty Blacks from St. Louis in a labor dispute at an aluminum factory. Most of the survivors were driven away.

St. Louis, the Gateway to the West, was once the thriving capital of the Southern Midwest. It was the Paris of the Prairie, which stretched endlessly from its very city limits. The elegance of the city and its women gave rise to painful scenes of jealousy from neighboring cities such as Memphis. Those lyrics of longing are set out in "St. Louis Blues":

> *I hate to see that evening sun go down*
> *I hate to see that evening sun go down*

'Cause my baby, he done left this town

Feeling tomorrow just like I feel today
Feeling tomorrow like I feel today
I'm gonna pack my bags and make my getaway

St. Louis woman with her diamond rings
She pulls my man around by her apron strings
And if it wasn't for powder and her store-bought hair
Oh, that man of mine, he wouldn't go nowhere, nowhere

I got that St. Louis blues, just as blue as I can be
My man's got a heart like a rock cast in the sea
Or else he wouldn't have gone so far from me

"St. Louis Blues"
William Christopher Handy, 1914

Detroit. Today there is a museum on East McLemore Avenue that relays this history. Booker T. Jones formed the band Booker T. and MGs here together with Steve Cropper, Duck Dunn and Al Jackson. The MGs were not British sports cars, but rather the Memphis Group, whose members were each exceptional instrumentalists. The Bar-Kays, Isaac Hayes, Albert King, B. B. King, Wilson Pickett, Otis Redding, Sam & Dave, The Staple Singers, Rufus Thomas and his daughter Carla recorded at Stax, often accompanied by the crisp sound of the Memphis Horns (Wayne Jackson and Andrew Low). Al Green produced his records here too, before his late calling in 1976 to serve as pastor at the Full Gospel Tabernacle Church in Memphis. In 1975, Stax went bankrupt. However, the Ardent label, founded in 1959, continues until today with stars like Sonic Youth, James Taylor, Townes Van Zandt, The White Stripes, and ZZ Top. But the magic sparked by Stax no longer lives on in Memphis. Rather, the city capitalizes on its musical past. Millions of visitors pay homage at Graceland and not a few of them expect a religious awakening there.

> *For reasons I cannot explain*
> *There's some part of me wants to see Graceland*
> *Maybe I've reason to believe*
> *We all will be received*
> *In Graceland*

"Graceland"
Paul Simon, 1986

While W.C. Handy has been appropriately honored, and Elvis gets all the hype, the greatest daughter of the city has been almost forgotten by her hometown.

Aretha Louise Franklin was born at 406 Lucy Avenue on

the preeminent blues tradition started by Chess with Willie Dixon and musicians like Muddy Waters, Howlin' Wolf, Little Walter, B. B. King and Chuck Berry, Phillips was increasingly drawn to White country and rock'n'roll musicians like Jerry Lee Lewis, Carl Perkins, Roy Orbison and Johnny Cash.

Marc Cohn saw Elvis Presley's ghost on Union Avenue. In "Guitar Man", Elvis sang about how hard the trip to Memphis was, and how much harder for a musician looking for work:

> *I hitchhiked all the way down to Memphis [...]*
>
> *For the next three weeks I went huntin' them nights*
> *Just lookin' for a place to play*
> *Well, I thought my pickin' would set 'em on fire*
> *But nobody wanted to hire a guitar man*

"Guitar Man"
Jerry Reed, 1967

Elvis had every reason to take trouble in stride. His first recordings at Sun Records in 1953 and 1954 launched his unparalleled career. While the Chicago label, Chess, stood for Black Chicago rhythm and blues and musicians like Chuck Berry or Memphis Slim, Sun Records in Memphis primarily represented White rock'n'roll and rockabilly. Elvis has Memphis to thank for his breakthrough and success. He spent his first fourteen years in Tupelo, Mississippi, before moving to Memphis. By 1957, he was a 22-year-old multi-millionaire. He built his fairy tale castle and mausoleum, Graceland, there, in Memphis.

The Memphis-based Stax label was one of the two most important producers of soul music, next to Motown in

And much earlier, in 1970, John Fogerty of Creedence Clearwater Revival was drawn to Memphis too:

> *737 coming out of the sky*
> *Won't you take me down to Memphis*
> *on a midnight ride*

"Travelin' Band"
John Fogerty, 1970

But some people, unlike Cohn, did not come to Memphis on a first-class ticket or by airplane at all:

> *I haven't eaten a bite*
> *Or slept for three days and nights*
> *That's how I got to Memphis*

"That's How I Got to Memphis"
Tom T. Hall, 1968

This is what Tom T. Hall, Bobby Bare, and Bill Haley sang in 1969. But why in the world did all these musicians want to go to Memphis in the first place? Because of Sam Phillips's great record label, Sun Records, of course. Phillips had worked at Chess in Chicago, but parted ways with the brothers Leonard and Phil Chess. So, he moved to Memphis in 1949 and founded Sun at 761 Union Avenue. (That's how he got to Memphis, that's how he got to Memphis.)

In the beginning, B. B. King, Howlin' Wolf, and Junior Parker were under contract. But Sun Studio soon started something new. In 1951 at Sun, Jackie Brenston recorded Ike Turner's "Rocket 88", which is generally considered the first rock'n'roll record. Instead of orienting his label toward

> *That melancholy strain, that ever-haunting refrain*
> *Is like a sweet old sorrow song*
> *Here comes the very part that wraps a spell*
>   *around my heart*
> *It sets me wild to hear that loving tune again*
> *The Memphis Blues*

"Memphis Blues"
William Christopher Handy, 1912

W.C. Handy does not enjoy immortal fame for "The Memphis Blues", but rather for his "St. Louis Blues". After his death in 1958, he received numerous honors. There was a biopic with Ella Fitzgerald and Nat King Cole called *St. Louis Blues*, the US Post Office issued a commemorative stamp, and in 1960 Handy Park was dedicated in strictly segregated Memphis to honor its famous son. It is located on Beale Street, not far from a weird Elvis Presley monument. The bald-headed composer and trumpet player casts a bit of an arrogant eye on you as he watches over, or should I say looks down on, his Beale Street, the holiest street connected to the blues.

> *W.C. Handy, won't you look down over me*
> *Yeah, I got a first-class ticket*
> *But I'm as blue as a boy can be*
>
> *Saw the ghost of Elvis*
> *On Union Avenue*
>
> *When I was walking in Memphis*
> *I was walking with my feet ten feet off of Beale*

"Walking in Memphis"
Marc Cohn, 1991

"written," they originated somehow and were played by many in variations and passed down as an oral history. Before Handy, there were not any blues composers, only a blues tradition. Secondly, Handy was Black. Not many African Americans were able to break through as composers and be recognized. But the third and most interesting thing is that W.C. Handy's most famous song is about St. Louis. Handy himself was from Memphis, and that is where he also wrote "St. Louis Blues."

In 1912, he had written "Memphis Blues", but it had limited success. Handy speaks of himself in the third person in this song as he sings his own praises. However, he sold the song rights for fifty dollars, with no royalties, to a Theron Bennett. So, in 1912, the pattern for pop music started: composers gave away their songs and others made a killing with them.

> *Folks I've just been down, down to Memphis town*
> *That's where the people smile, smile on you all the while*
> *Hospitality, they were good to me*
> *I couldn't spend a dime and had the grandest time*
>
> *I went out a dancing with a Tennessee dear*
> *They had a fellow there named Handy*
> *   with a band you should hear*
> *And while the folks gently swayed,*
> *   all the band folks played real harmony*
> *I never will forget the tune that Handy called*
> *   the Memphis Blues*
> *Oh yes, them blues*
>
> *There's nothing like the Handy Band*
> *   that played the Memphis Blues so grand*
> *Oh, play them blues*

MEMPHIS

I hate to see that evening sun go down
I hate to see that evening sun go down
Cause my baby, he done left this town

St. Louis woman with her diamon' rings
Pulls that man around by her apron strings
If it wasn't for powder and for store-bought hair
The man I love, he would not go nowhere, nowhere

Got the St. Louis blues, blue as I can be
My man got a heart like a rock in the sea
Or else he wouldn't go so far from me

"St. Louis Blues"
William Christopher Handy, 1915

"St. Louis Blues" is one of the first blues compositions written down on paper. Trumpet player and composer, William Christopher Handy, was forty years old when he wrote the song in 1914. There are three unusual things about this song. First, until then blues songs were not

March 25, 1942. While no one contests her title as the Queen of Soul, it is interesting to note that her father, Clarence LaVaughn, recorded even more records than she did. However, it was recorded sermons that made the Baptist preacher famous. Aretha Franklin, who died in August 2018, has been called the best vocalist of all time by many critics. Sadly, her birth home has long been abandoned, though there is talk of renovations. Memphis has numerous other attractions and musical memorials, but Aretha Franklin is not associated with the city of her birth. She moved with her parents to Detroit when she was two years old.

Especially when circumstances are less than happy, one likes to project oneself into an idyllic alternative world. Then, music becomes a realm of its own, a refuge:

> *They're not showing any lights tonight [...]*
> *There's just a hot-blooded singer*
> *Singing Memphis in June*

> "Tight Connection to My Heart"
> Bob Dylan, 1985

The here mentioned "Memphis in June" delves into the fiction of the good old days (for Whites, at least) and sleepy small-town life:

> *A shade veranda under Sunday blue sky*
> *And my cousin Miranda, she's making a blueberry pie*
>
> *Everything so peaceful and dandy*
> *I can see my grandmama 'cross the street, still a-rocking*
> *Watching all the neighbors go by*

> *Sweet oleander blowing perfume in the air everywhere*
> *It's paradise take my advice*
> *'Cos there's nothing like old Memphis in June*

"Memphis in June"
Carmichael/Webster, 1945

When Hoagy Carmichael and Paul Francis Webster published this song, they struck a nerve. No one had ever described better an idyllic Southern lazy Sunday afternoon on the front porch when time slows down, the smells intoxicate, and pies are baking. The only song that even comes close is "Georgia on My Mind", also by Carmichael but a different lyricist. Also, maybe "Clyde" by J.J. Cale is a contender. But that's another story.

Carmichael doesn't even come from the South, he was a lawyer from Indiana who listened to a tip from a friend who said, "Nobody ever lost money writing songs about the South."

But now back to Marc Cohn's "Walking in Memphis": Did he have too much awe for the greats to be able to walk directly on legendary Beale Street? Perhaps he is trying to show ten feet of respect?

> *Then I'm walking in Memphis*
> *Walking with my feet ten feet off of Beale*

These are the lyrics of Handy's "Beale Street Blues":

> *If Beale Street could talk, if Beale Street could talk*
> *Married men would have to take their beds and walk*
> *Except one or two, who never drink booze*
> *And the blind man on the corner*
> *Who sings the Beale Street Blues*

> *He said, "I'd rather be there than any place I know*
> *Yes, I'd rather be here than any place I know*
> *It's gonna take the sergeant for to make me go"*
>
> *I'm goin' to the river maybe by and by*
> *Yes, I'm goin' to the river, and there's a reason why*
> *Because the river's wet, and Beale Street's*
>   *done gone dry*

"Beale Street Blues"
William Christopher Handy, 1916

Louis Armstrong made his famous recording of the song in 1954, but it seems like Handy had a nostalgic view of Beale Street even before that happened. Larger Beale Street, Memphis's big entertainment district and home to dozens of blues and rockabilly clubs still looks like it did in the 1950s when Albert Williams sang about it. This is another song about arriving, about getting there. It gives an impression of how tightly knit the brotherhood of blues musicians used to be. Just walk into any joint in Memphis and you will find your fellow blues cats there:

> *You know, when I first got to Memphis*
> *I went out on Thomas Street*
> *With all the talking about Johnny Curtis's night club*
>
> *I see old Joe Williams there*
> *I looked over in the corner I saw Nick*
> *I look way behind me, there was James*

"Rhumba Chillen"
Albert Williams, 1953

What sets the music scene of Memphis apart from other

cities in the South, and what is really special, is the tradition of jug bands. Willie Shade, who was born in 1898 in Memphis, founded the first one, called Memphis Jug Band. In the mid-1920s, Shade was nicknamed Brimmer by his friends after his grandmother Annie Brimmer. And that's how he was known as leader for the Memphis Jug Band and the founder of the jug band tradition. The Memphis Jug Band was the most popular jug band in America between 1927-1934. Brimmer sang and played a homemade one string bass, guitar, and harmonica. Singers would hold a jug, jar, can or bowl below their mouths to sing into to increase their resonance while they were vocally imitating instruments. Jug band music is the *arte povera* of African American music. Brimmer also played with the Memphis Sanctified Singers.

The second doyen of jug band music was Charlie Burse, and he often played with Brimmer in ever changing line-ups. Burse recorded with the very successful Victor and Brunswick labels. Word quickly spread to other record labels about this trend, and they rushed to Memphis to record more jug band tracks. This resulted in a thriving jug band scene in Memphis in the 1920s and '30s. The Perfect label signed the singer Jack Kelley's South Memphis Jug Band. And Vocalion had a contract with Al Jackson's Beale Street Jug Band. But the best band was the Jug Stompers lead by Gus Cannon. They recorded "Feather Bed", perhaps the best jug band disc of all time. The song stands out for its clear social commentary on the end of slavery, Jim Crow, and racism:

> *I remember the time just before the war*
> *Colored man used to fuss about shucks and straw*
> *But now, bless God, old massa dead*

> *Colored man plumb fool about feather bed*

"Feather Bed"
Cannon's Jug Stompers, 1928

Gus Cannon and Hosie Woods also founded the band, Cannon and Woods—The Beale Street Boys, and recorded the song "Fourth and Beale" together. Then the Memphis Jug Band played in changing line-ups that went by the names of Memphis Sheiks, Carolina Peanut Boys, or Charlie Burse and His Memphis Mudcats. Brimmer's music helped forge skiffle music in late 1950s England. Brimmer died of pneumonia in Memphis in 1966.

Beale Street, the center of blues and jug band music In Memphis, is just a 20-minute walk from the Lorraine Motel at 450 Mulberry Street where Reverend Dr. Martin Luther King Jr. was shot by James Earl Ray on the hotel balcony of room of 306 on April 4, 1968.

> *Were you there when the man from Atlanta*
> *was murdered in Memphis?*
> *Did you see him layin' at the Lorraine Motel?*
>
> *Run and tell somebody there's blood on the riverside*
> *If you were there, you'd swear it was more than*
> *a man who died*

"Motel in Memphis"
Old Crow Medicine Show, 2008

It was not just the man Martin Luther King Jr. of Atlanta who was slain. It was also the civil rights movement itself that was shot down in Memphis:

> *Another man from Atlanta, Georgia*

> *By name of Martin Luther King*
> *He shook the land like the rolling thunder*
> *And made the bells of freedom ring today*
> *With a dream of beauty that they could not burn away*

"They Killed Him"
Kris Kristofferson, 1985

The belief that peaceful protest could lead to societal change also died in Memphis. More than a man, a whole universe had collapsed. After the assassination of MLK, the struggle briefly radicalized then died down. The movement recently flared back up after the killings of Michael Brown and George Floyd, and Black Lives Matter led to mass protest and brought millions onto the streets.

The Lorraine Motel is just a few steps from the Mississippi River, near Tom Lee Park. Tom Lee was a Black resident and hero. After a boat accident in 1925, he single-handedly saved 32 passengers from drowning although he himself could not swim. In 1997 Jeff Buckley did drown in Memphis in the Mississippi. The monument to Tom Lee was destroyed by a storm, a storm which was, absurdly, named "Elvis." Tom Lee Park lies above the Mississippi River and offers a wide vista across the river to Arkansas. It is close to where little Marie, who was made famous by Chuck Berry, lived:

> *Her home is on the Southside, high upon a ridge*
> *Just a half a mile from the Mississippi Bridge*

"Memphis, Tennessee"
Chuck Berry, 1959

The location of Marie's home can be clearly identified.

The south riverbank on the Tennessee side is the only place that fits the description: a half a mile from the bridge and on a ridge. On that ridge you can still find the South Bluff Apartments, luxury homes and condominiums line the top of the bluff overlooking the park and the river. But it seems certain that little, Black Marie never lived in such luxury. When Berry wrote "Memphis, Tennessee" in 1959, he must have known the modest African American world of Marie had long fallen victim to extensive redevelopment that created the park and luxury apartments for Whites.

> *Help me, information, more than that I cannot add*
> *Only that I miss her and all the fun we had*

> "Memphis, Tennessee"
> Chuck Berry, 1959

The narrator doesn't just yearn for little Marie but also the lost world of Memphis, Tennessee, "on the Southside, high upon a ridge, just a half a mile from the Mississippi Bridge." More than a girl had been lost, a world had collapsed. Before I understood this context, I thought the song "Memphis, Tennessee" was a somewhat immature and unsettling love song. But where did Chuck Berry come from? From St. Louis, naturally. Memphis and St. Louis were and will always be connected, just like in the work of W.C. Handy.

ACKNOWLEDGMENTS

I would like to thank Amy Kardel, M.J. Williams, Wilbert Harrison and Hal Hartley. And I would like to dedicate this book to the memory of Ralph Bethke, a real gone cat.

www.ingramcontent.com/pod-product-compliance
Lightning Source LLC
Chambersburg PA
CBHW071339080526
44587CB00017B/2895